WHEN DEATH COMES KNOCKING FOR YOUR PATIENTS

When Death Comes Knocking for Your Patients:
A Guide for Nurses and Palliative Caregivers

First Published in the USA in 2017 by Peacock Proud Press
ISBN 978-0-9981212-6-0 paperback
ISBN 978-0-9981212-7-7 eBook

Library of Congress Control Number: 2017953361

Book Cover and Interior Design:
Melinda Tipton Martin, MartinPublishingServices.com

Portrait Photographer:
Carolyn Mae, carolynmaephotography.com

Editors:
Laura L. Bush, Ph.D., laurabushphd.com
Evelyn Jeffries, Elegant Editing
Wendy Ledger, VoType Transcription and Editing Services

DISCLAIMER:
This is a work of nonfiction. The information is of a general nature to help readers know and understand more about palliative caregiving. Readers of this publication agree that Meina J. Dubetz will not be held responsible or liable for damages that may be alleged or resulting directly or indirectly from their use of this publication. All external links are provided as a resource only and are not guaranteed to remain active for any length of time. The author cannot be held accountable for the information provided by, or actions resulting from accessing these resources.

WHEN D·E·A·T·H COMES KNOCKING FOR YOUR PATIENTS

A GUIDE FOR NURSES AND PALLIATIVE CAREGIVERS

MEINA J. DUBETZ, RN

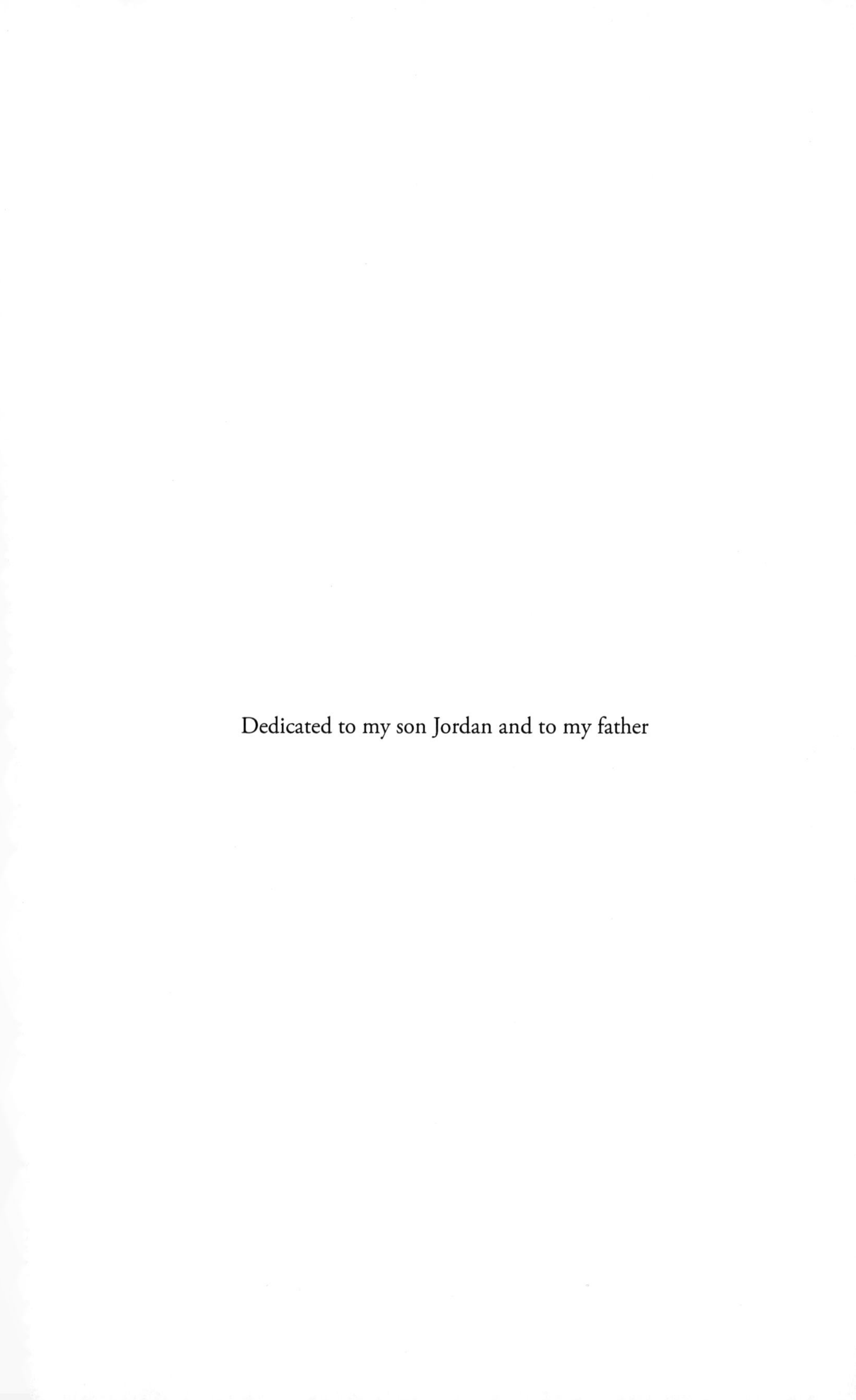
Dedicated to my son Jordan and to my father

Endorsements and Advanced Praise

Meina Dubetz has written a powerful book filled with her own personal experiences and the knowledge she has gained during her nursing career. *When Death Comes Knocking for Your Patients* is an excellent resource and a valuable tool for the new healthcare professional in Palliative care. It's also a reminder about why many of us entered this corridor of nursing many years ago.

– Diane Jahraus RN, BScN, CON(C)
Charge Nurse, Radiation Oncology Nursing

When Death Comes Knocking for Your Patients is extremely powerful and moving. The author's heartfelt wisdom gently provides guidance and support to readers, nurses, and family members as they move along their journey with death and grief. This book allowed me to explore my own various emotions related to life and death. I had goose bumps throughout and couldn't put it down.

– Katelyn Callander RN, BN
Graduating Class 2017, University of Calgary

Real, relatable, and relevant. Meina Dubetz shares deeply moving, often agonizing stories from her career as an oncology and palliative care nurse, as well as her experiences as a daughter, mother, family member, and friend. *When Death Comes Knocking for Your Patients* will captivate readers while educating them on death and dying. Dubetz tackles tough topics, such as crossing professional boundaries, medical assistance in dying, and caring for a dying colleague. She also offers practical, tangible solutions and suggestions for the inevitable and innumerable challenges that arise when caring for patients and their loved ones as death approaches. Included are profound lessons for novice and experienced nurses alike, but those lessons are not limited to health care providers. The ubiquity of death makes this a must read for anyone.

– Reanne Booker, MN BScN NP
Palliative and End-of-Life Services, Alberta Health Services

I enjoyed reading *When Death Comes Knocking for Your Patients.* The book offers great value for caregivers and for patients and their families.

– Dr. Srini Chary, MBBS, MRCS; LRCP, CCFP (PC), DA, FRCSEd.
Consulting Physician, Regional Palliative & Hospice Care, Calgary Zone
Palliative Medicine, Clinical Assistant Professor,
Department of Oncology & Family Medicine,
Cummings School of Medicine, University of Calgary

This two-part book about dying and death is based on Meina Dubetz's profound personal experiences as a nurse for over 30 years. Cleverly separated into two sections—the first section on care for others and the second section on care for oneself—the book provides many important and useful tips about how to cope with dying and death in a more dignified, graceful, and human way. Well worth the read!

– Stephen Garrett, MA
Death Educator and Author of
When Death Speaks, Listen, Learn, and Love

CONTENTS

Acknowledgements

This book would not be possible without the support and love of the following people in my life:

Stephen Garrett—Author, Death coach and advocate. You gave me "permission" to move my thoughts from someday to now. Thank you for your endorsement and encouragement.

Laura Bush—Editor, Publisher and Author. You have an ability to reach inside my mind and show me how to articulate my thoughts. You are not only my editor and publisher; you are a mentor, teacher and now a friend. You cleared my runway so I could take flight.

My family, my husband Art, children Darcy, Kelsey (Jai), Jordana and grandchildren Jayden, Jake, Ever and Dalen, my mom Agnes – you are the reason my life is filled with joy.

Marg deVries—My cousin. In my darkest days, it was you who held out a candle of light.

To the rest of my family, and my friends, thank you for your ongoing love and support.

Lori Bashutski—You supported me from day one by providing an inspiring environment to write my first draft. You are never short of uplifting words and time to talk.

Cathie Godfrey—Fellow author, friend, and weekly on-line support. Thank you for your insights. and listening to me as a fellow writer.

My girl friends – Bev Keeler, Deb Legal and Ginny Holm – you are the sisters I never had.

The Wisdom Community of Landmark Worldwide—Jerry Fishman, Chip, Ginny, Lori, Wendy, Joshua, Christine, Dave, Emily, Bruce, Joanne, Stephanie and more. It was through your listening of me as an author that I have become one.

Phil Mitchell, Natasha LeBlanc, Karen, and Randy Kermack—Thank you for the music you played while I danced with your loved ones. I am blessed to continue the dance with you.

INTRODUCTION

WHEN DEATH CAME KNOCKING IN MY LIFE

I am watching over all you do,
Another child you will bear.
Believe me when I say to you,
That I am always there.
Although I've never breathed your air
Or gazed into your eyes,
That doesn't mean I never was.
A memory never dies.

—*Revised from original by unknown author*

JORDAN

The first time I heard Death knock, it was not for me or one of my patients. It was for my baby. For nine months, I carried this little miracle and all the dreams I had for him. Two days after his due date, he stopped moving. Concerned and a little frightened, I called the doctor. He urged me to come into the hospital immediately. My husband and I made the 20-minute car ride in silence. He was deep in his thoughts and I in mine. The admitting desk instructed me to go to the maternity unit, where they admitted me right away. Once I was in the room, a nurse started the intravenous drip to challenge the baby's activity and assess his response.

The nursing staff sent my husband home, and I was left in my room with a fetal heart monitor strapped around my belly. My nurse dimmed the lights and told me to rest. Surprisingly, I dozed off. The steady sound of my baby's heartbeat over the monitor reassured me that all was well. Then a piercing alarm startled me awake. The door to my room flew open, and three nurses ran into the room. They glanced at the monitor, disconnected the straps, kicked the emergency brake off my bed, and rushed me down to the Ultrasound Department.

Anxiously, I watched as the technician lubricated my belly and began rolling the probe back and forth. Even though I was a nurse, I hadn't been trained to assess what I was seeing on the screen. I couldn't even distinguish my baby's head from his bottom. At the time, I would have given anything for someone in the room to offer me any words of comfort that my baby was okay. Instead, I saw the technician glance over to the radiologist, who lowered his eyes and shook his head.

Once I saw that, they didn't need to tell me what they were seeing. I had seen that same look before when doctors stopped CPR after they had no more hope.

"Please, no!" I cried.

The radiologist reached over, touched my hand, and said, "I am so sorry."

I refused to believe him. He had to be mistaken. I was not going to give up. I would deliver a perfect baby and prove them all wrong.

The umbilical cord had a knot in it and was wrapped three times around Jordan's little neck. As the resident doctor delivered my baby, I could hear the medical staff whispering, "stillborn." Oh, how I hate that cold term: "stillborn." It sounded as though they were saying that in spite of everything, he "still" managed to be born. Over the years, my own language about this term changed. I began referring to my son's birth as "born still"—delivered quietly and peacefully. After realizing my baby was gone, I felt heartbroken. This perfect little boy with beautiful auburn hair and little pouty kissable lips would never have a chance to experience the love of his parents, never play with his brother and sister, and never meet the many people who were anxiously awaiting his arrival.

While the nurses were busy cleaning up the delivery room, I remember the resident telling me, "That was the first time I had to deliver a stillborn."

"Me, too," I said.

I don't remember if she said anything more to me after that confession, although I realize now she was probably reaching out to connect with me somehow—to say this experience was difficult for her, too. But I didn't care about her personal medical experiences or how hard this first experience with a baby's death was on her. Did she expect an apology from me for having put her through this? That's what it sounded like to me at the time. I didn't respond to what she told me, refusing her any comfort in my time of need.

Immediately after my baby's delivery, the nurses whisked me off to a non-maternity ward filled with every noise except the crying of babies and the excited chatter of new mothers. I lay for hours in a room all by myself with no one to assess my fundus to confirm that my uterus was contracting after delivery, no one to check my flow to ensure I was not hemorrhaging, and no one to assess how I was coping. I felt I was being punished for the ultimate crime, and no one wanted anything to do with me.

Around 3:00 a.m., I crept out of my room and quietly tiptoed down the hallway. Peeking around the corner, I could see five nurses sitting around their station, knitting and laughing. Obviously, their workload wasn't keeping them from checking on me. No longer caring if they heard me or not, I went back into my room and sat for another hour. Finally, I could not stand the isolation anymore. I needed to speak to someone—anyone—so I rang the bell and asked for a Tylenol that I didn't even need. A nurse very efficiently brought it to me.

"There you go," she said, as she placed it on the bedside table.

I watched her avoid eye contact with me and bustle out of the room as though she had a million other things to do. It was obvious she had drawn the short straw and couldn't wait to get back to a comfortable environment away from death.

After enduring these insensitivities in the hospital, I was discharged home first thing in the morning. No one set up a postnatal nursing home visit for me. After all, I hadn't gone home with a baby in my arms, so no one needed to assess my well-being—or so they thought.

Feeling numb and removed from the rest of the world, I went through the motions of a private funeral service, spreading Jordan's small amount of ashes on the property of the little lone church that sat just a few miles outside of Calgary where I had married my child's daddy.

My arms ached with longing to hold my baby.

People tried their best to connect with me, stumbling through words of comfort. But they could not do or say anything that would pull me out of my deep despair. My husband was trying to cope with and process his own loss. Soon, and sadly, we each detached ourselves from our marriage, emotionally separated by our individual grief.

I robotically continued to care for my other two children and everyday chores, but I felt removed and dispassionate about life. The world outside kept moving. At times, I wanted to scream, "Stop! My baby has died. Just stop and feel my pain!" No one understood, nor could they. I was stumbling on this dark road by myself.

During my six-week postpartum visit with my family doctor, I told him I couldn't seem to break through this heavy cloud of sadness—and sometimes anger—that kept me from moving forward with my life. I was experiencing deep sadness about my baby's unfulfilled future. I felt such rage at the doctor on call that night—a specialist who had not bothered to leave the comfort of his bed to come and assess me. Perhaps had he personally examined me, it could have made a difference. He might have said, "Let's do a C-section just to be safe."

But I had no C-section that night, and now, I had no baby.

My family doctor suggested seeing a counselor. He ended our visit by reaching into his lab coat and producing a check for the amount of money I had paid for the "Obstetric fee" he charged. I looked at it as a refund for an incomplete contract. At the time, I'm not sure who felt worse: my doctor with his own unspoken remorse or me for taking the money.

A few days later, I went for my counseling appointment. The receptionist ushered me in to the room where an elderly psychiatrist peered over his half-framed glasses and asked me, "So what brings you in today?

I first thought, "Did you not prepare for our meeting and read the referral letter?"

I then thought, "How can you, as a man, possibly know what I am feeling or going through?"

I felt no connection with him. He had his pen poised above his yellow pad of lined paper, waiting for my answer.

I took a deep breath and asked, "Have you ever lost a child?"

"No," he said.

"Then I don't think you can possibly relate to what I'm feeling or going through."

He mumbled something about techniques of coping with grief. I stood up, thanked him for his time, and left. There was no way I could open myself up and share my grief about my son's death with someone who was speaking from a textbook and not from his heart.

When I got home, I called my cousin. Marg had lost a baby boy, Adam, the year before. She invited me to come over. That first visit began what became regular meetings together over coffee to share our grief and experiences. Marg understood my raw grief, my sadness, and my pain. She allowed me to cry openly. I had finally found someone who could relate to what I was experiencing. I will be forever grateful to her for opening up her old wounds, so she could help me heal mine.

Looking back, I can now see that a referral to a support group would have been more beneficial for me rather than a psychiatric appointment. I was paralyzed by grief and needed a connection with someone I could relate to who understood—someone to tell me that what I was feeling was normal.

Over the next few months, my journey with death and grief became easier. The pain in my heart became less torturous. I felt I could breathe deeper and allow a little more of life in every day. The dark clouds moved away, and the ache in my arms became more bearable. My pendulum of emotions still swung from occasional anger to depression. For a little while, I would accept the loss of my baby. Then I'd be back again feeling angry or sad. More months passed. Eventually, the swing of my emotions stabilized and found a new mark. I felt more resilient and able to cope. I could see that my experience with grief could very easily remain bottled up within me, keeping me from living powerfully, or I could do something constructive with my pain.

I made a decision to return to school and become an oncology nurse. I had survived a life-altering journey that could make a difference for others who were going through their own confusion and disbelief about an unexpected death or life-threatening situation.

I wrote this book so I could share with nurses who are new to palliative care what I have learned working with terminally ill patients. My 30 years of professional and personal experience with end-of-life events have taught me how to connect, interact with, and care for terminally ill patients. I hope my experiences and sharing my knowledge and skills will help nurses, hospice care workers, and death doulas enhance the care they deliver for their patients, the patients' families and friends, and make a difference.

QUESTIONS TO ASK YOURSELF

1. When have you experienced the loss of someone close to you? What was your reaction? Where did you go for support? What inspired you? If you have not encountered the death of a loved one, share your thoughts about what you think it might be like to experience this.

2. What do you think the resident doctor and the nurses could have said to you that would have given you support?

3. If you had been the nurse on duty and entered my room with the Tylenol, could you have spent some time talking to me? What would you say? On the other hand, do you think you would need to escape to a more comfortable environment?

PART I

DELIVERING COMPASSIONATE CARE TO YOUR PATIENTS AT THE END OF LIFE

Because I could not stop for Death—
He kindly stopped for me—
The Carriage held but just Ourselves—
And Immortality.

Emily Dickinson

CHAPTER 1

FEARING DEATH AND THE DARK VOID OF DEMENTIA

The mind is everything.
What you think, you become.

—*Buddha*

AFTER READING THIS CHAPTER

You will be able to connect with your patient as a human being with a life history.

You will recognize the struggles and difficulties families face when their family members are only a shell of who they once were.

THE FIRST MAN I LOVED

My father was born in the Netherlands in 1927. His mother had raised him and his three siblings on her own, after her husband died from a bleeding ulcer at the young age of 42. Money was always scarce, and my grandmother struggled to make ends meet. One of my father's sisters was handicapped, adding to the financial and emotional burden of the family. One year my father was forced to wear his mother's old shoes to school. He never forgot how his classmates humiliated and teased him.

Dad left school after the sixth grade and went to work as a farmhand. As far as he was concerned, having money was the only way he could prove himself. He joined the Dutch army when he was 18 years old. Enlisting gave him a sense of security as well as an opportunity for adventure. He was shipped off to Indonesia after a year of training, leaving my mother wearing an engagement ring and holding his promise to return.

My father never discussed any aspect of what he did in the Army. As children, we sometimes asked, "Did you ever shoot anyone?" He would take a moment to answer and then say, "No, nothing like that." We suspected that there was more to the story than he was prepared to share with us. We asked our mother about what happened, but he didn't speak to her about his experiences either.

What she did say was that the man who came back two years later was a different man from the one who had left. He returned filled with adventure and a hunger to see and do more in the world. She had waved goodbye to a boy and a man returned. Going back to life in a small town driving a truck was no longer enough for my father. He dreamed of immigrating to Canada. This vision motivated him to work even harder and drive longer hours to save the money to fulfill his dream.

A few years passed before my father's dream became reality. During one of those years, he married my mother. A year later, I arrived. By the time I was almost three, my parents had the necessary documents, enough money saved, and a few personal items packed for our great adventure to Canada.

Canada was the land of opportunity, and my dad's dreams were high. He was not discouraged with having to work as a farmhand for a few years. The time allowed him to save enough money to begin his own concrete company. Once he had established his business, he focused totally on his work. He would spend long hours at job sites ensuring that the concrete he set was hardening perfectly. As the years went by, he became more successful. The more the company grew, the less time Dad spent with his family. I felt disconnected from him. Many of our conversations ended with him frustrated and me in tears. I moved out of our family home at 18. I doubted anyone would miss me. At the time I left, my brothers were 4 and 14 years old. I knew they weren't aware of the situation or my feelings.

The summer after I moved out, I went to work in an old-age care facility as a nursing attendant, visiting my parents at least once during the week. As time passed, I felt a shift in how my father related to me. He had always said that hard work showed character. Since I was now part of the work force, he showed new respect for me. Now he appeared to listen to me as someone who had something worth sharing.

I ended up telling my parents some of the sad details of my work. For example, I told them how several of my patients were not even aware of where they were, let alone what day it was. These patients were receiving basic care from inadequately trained personnel like me. They were sitting in that facility just waiting to die. "No one comes to visit them," I told my mom and dad. "They are The Forgotten."

That was when my father told me his greatest fear was ending up forgotten in a nursing home, demented and no longer able to make his wishes known. "If that happens," he said, "shoot me."

In 2001, his greatest fear became reality. A series of little strokes slowly took away most of his memory and his ability to live safely at home. My two brothers and I found it very difficult to deal with my mother's guilt about this situation. She had promised to be with my father through sickness and in health, which for her included personally providing the care he needed. Unfortunately, she could not see that her own health was at stake by giving him all of her attention. She became weak and fatigued by lack of sleep because my father would spend most of his nights wandering through the house. He would spend hours in his recliner napping during the day while my mom cleaned and prepared meals. She was giving him 24-hour support. We were afraid we'd lose her, too.

When the home care nurse or the geriatric physician came to assess my father, I would make sure I was there. My dad did not know his surroundings anymore. Every time he would walk out of his bedroom, he would look around in amazement as if seeing his home for the first time. Even though he was not aware of his environment, he would astound us with his ability to remember when he was going to be assessed.

"Is the nurse coming?" he would ask. When he heard she was, he would then ask to see the newspaper. It didn't take long for us to figure out why. He would look at the date of the newspaper and memorize it, so he could give the correct date when a staff member gave him a cognitive exam to assess his memory

I could see that even in his demented mind he was able to figure some things out. He knew, for example, that he needed to get the answers right. I don't think he realized what passing or failing meant, but he did know that he had to offer the right answer to win this game he was forced to play.

My concern about my mother's well-being increased. She was my father's primary caregiver, and I watched her energy and appetite decline. My father wandered through the house at nights, often getting lost. Mom would wake up to him yelling, "Where am I?" Sometimes she would find him in the basement in the spare room or in the furnace room, not being able to figure out that he needed to take the stairs to get back to his own bedroom. He was walking around as if his own home was a maze. My mother would be afraid to fall back to sleep again, which made her sleep deprived. Her once encouraging words to return to bed left her irritated whenever he refused. She felt frustrated and then guilty for her lack of patience with her husband.

I had a heartbreaking conversation with my mother when I told her we needed to move Dad to a facility where he could be cared for best. In her mind, she thought she was managing and doing the best she could. My brothers and I finally had to tell her that we were afraid she would die before Dad because he was draining all her energy.

We had attempted to provide Mom with some respite care by having our father spend a few hours or even a few days away from home.

However, she only felt more anxious when she was separated from him. Even taking my mother out for lunch was not helpful. I found it easier to take her back early rather than watch Mom constantly look at her watch. I knew her heart was home with my father.

The very difficult day came when we moved Dad from his family home to a nursing home. My brothers and I felt guilty moving our father out of his home and physically separating him from the woman he had lived with for more than 53 years. Dad always admired doctors, so it was easy to convince him to leave the house for a medical assessment over a few days. Eager to please his physician, Dad actually seemed excited as we packed up some of his belongings.

Watching my mom hold back her tears, knowing that her husband would never come home again, was devastating.

"It's for the best, Mom," we told her.

But best for whom? Certainly not my mom, since she just wanted nothing more than to have her husband at home with her.

Integrating him into another place to live would have its challenges. We were well aware that the story we had told my father about the doctors needing to evaluate him would only work for so long.

Our city's home-care system required families to take the first facility with an available bed. Once he was admitted, we could request a transfer. However, we could not understand moving a patient with dementia twice. Once was upsetting enough. Why do this to him again? Having my father settle in was our top priority; we would not be disrupting him any more than necessary. Therefore, we endured the worn, outdated furniture from the 1970s, the smell of incontinence, the patients who shuffled around aimlessly, and the general hopeless energy of this first facility. Knowing that Dad was no longer aware of a room's décor made having him there, even for a short time, easier for us to bear.

Visiting every day was difficult for my mother because she had to drive half an hour to see her husband. We had hoped he could be admitted to a nursing home five minutes from their house, but the health care system didn't care about that. The rules were in place for a reason—but not for the right reason, as far as we were concerned.

My 79-year-old mother drove daily down a major freeway to visit her husband. If the speed and congestion of the traffic did not tax her nerves, my father's constant inquiries about when he could go home did. We were grateful my father was still aware we were his family members, but he could not grasp why he was not at home. The earlier story we told him about the doctor needing to evaluate him had lost its effectiveness. We had to tell him the truth.

"This is your home now, Dad."

The news tipped the scale of our father's already suspicious mind.

"Is someone else in Mom's life," he asked us. "Is that why you're keeping me here?"

We tried our best to ease his fears, but he became more withdrawn and less communicative. My mother tried her best to explain what was happening, but often by the time she told him, he was already on a different thought wave and no longer listening.

Three weeks after he was admitted, our family got together to celebrate his 77th birthday. We brought in a chocolate birthday cake, his favorite, and invited some of the residents to sit around the dining room table with us to share in the celebration. My dad was the center of attention. He was in his glory. We sang "Happy Birthday" and watched him blow out the candles. In our hearts, each of us knew that this would be the last time we would be celebrating his birthday with him.

Then, among all the laughter and the cutting of the cake, one of the residents, with a weak frail voice, started to sing in German. Instantly, my family witnessed my father's face change from smiling and joyful to staring straight ahead at this lady who was singing. His eyes bore into her when he suddenly shouted at her "Just shut up!" Instantly, in his mind, his loving family no longer surrounded him. Instead, he was imprisoned in a Nazi concentration camp. As far as we knew, Dad was never a prisoner of war. We were certain that he had heard stories from other soldiers about the war camps. Just hearing the stories must have terrified our father enough for those thoughts to stay in his subconscious mind. The innocent German song tipped the scale.

This fear stayed with him for several weeks. He was always looking for an opportunity to sneak out of the building. The staff applied a monitor to his wrist that would set off an alarm if he made it through the front door. He was successful many times. The nursing team would run out and bring him back into the building. When we would visit my father, he asked us how we got in. Then he would beg us to get out while we could. He thought we were also in the camp with him. We could not persuade him otherwise.

I remember one day I was trying to convince my father that he was safe and not in a concentration camp. He looked at me as if I had been brainwashed, then took my hand, and we walked down a hall. He stopped outside one of the resident's rooms, pointing at the dry eraser board outside the door. The staff wrote messages here, and you could see the current dates of nurses on duty on these boards. When I saw a message on this board written in German, I was shocked. The message was obviously to orientate a resident in his or her native language, but to my father, the German words provided clear evidence that he was, in fact, a prisoner of war.

Daily we witnessed our father's anxious, depressed thinking. He became distrustful and adamantly refused to take any of his routine medications. The nurses then began to hide his pills in his food. For a few days, that worked. My father's paranoia then escalated. He began to question the food. No amount of encouragement, even from his family, would change his mind. He refused to eat. It was if he instinctively knew that there was something not right, and the safest way for him was not to eat. Our family even brought in some of his favorite dishes, hoping he would trust us, and that the familiar cooking would encourage him. He remained paranoid and would shout, "They want to poison me!"

We asked the nursing staff what else could be done. They suggested using a feeding tube, but that would require more active nursing care and could not be provided in a nursing home. He would have to be admitted into a hospital. I was aware that it would be a temporary solution. It would only be a matter of time before he pulled out the tube, and then he would be restrained. As a nurse, I knew that restraints usually caused more aggravation and aggression.

The situations were difficult. In order to keep him alive, we would be subjecting him to a different level of fear—strapping him down and confining his movements. We saw the choice he had made. In his own way, my father had decided what would be best for him.

When confused patients like my father do not trust their caregivers, sometimes keeping the same staff members caring for them can minimize a patient's fear and paranoia. I saw that my father's caregivers were using this method with friendly "hellos" when they walked into the room and calling him by his first name, as if they had known each other for years, which made him smile back. But I could also always see the leeriness in his eyes, observing their every move.

My family members felt heartbroken watching this once vibrant, brilliant man slowly lose the last fragments of his mental faculties. I could not imagine the nightmare reality he was living. I would sit holding his hand, watching his face, seeing him try to figure out what was going on. All the anatomy classes I had taken about the human brain never taught me how unpredictable an individual's cerebral intelligence could be. I realized my dad's mind had become his worst enemy.

Eventually, my father's plan to escape became more aggressive. As he stood near the end of the hall next to the kitchen, a nurse approached him. He hit her across the face, pushing her out of his way. He then grabbed a mop from a nearby cleaning pail and began to swing it around as other staff members moved toward him. He ended up cornering four staff members, threatening them by continuing to swing his weapon of choice.

The unit supervisor called me to come immediately because the staff could not control my father. The drive was emotional for me since I knew the staff had to protect themselves. They would have to move my father to a facility for more unmanageable patients. I arrived to witness my dad's aggressive behavior. My brother had arrived a little earlier, and got dad to put down the mop. He had also managed to persuade dad to take some apple juice that held a sedative. Unfortunately, he was still uncooperative and stood his ground, refusing to return to his room.

That left the staff no other alternative. They prepared an injection of Haldol (a sedative) and as the nurse returned with the syringe, three other staff members moved toward my father. I helped hold him as we eased my father down to the floor. He was swinging his arms and kicking his feet. A nurse quickly and efficiently gave him the injection in his right hip. Restraining my own father, like some out-of-control animal, was one of the most difficult things I ever had to do.

Finally, my father slept, either from the Haldol, pure exhaustion, or from the relief of escaping his nightmarish reality. I sat on the floor next to him, rhythmically rubbing his back and humming "Danny Boy," his favorite song. A staff member brought a pillow and blanket for my father, whispering to me that they would help move him to his bed when he was more deeply sedated.

I sat and watched his breathing, wondering what I could learn from my father's end-of-life journey. Certainly, he was no longer capable of gaining any more of life's lessons. I questioned God and His "plan." Then I asked God just to take my father peacefully.

My brother left to pick up my mother. By the time, they returned, the staff had transferred my father back to his room. The three of us sat together watching my father sleeping soundly while we whispered to each other, "What happens now? They can't sedate him forever."

A few hours later, we had our answer. The nurse in charge came into the room and motioned for us to step into the hallway to speak to her. I appreciated that she did not speak to us in front of my father. I believe that, regardless of someone's body being in a sedated state, a person's mind is still capable of hearing. My brother and I stepped into the hallway, leaving my mother to sit with her husband, holding his hand. The charge nurse told us how sorry she was that my father's situation had escalated and that there was no longer any choice but to move him to another facility. We understood that his uncontrollable behavior did not meet the criteria to remain where he was.

I had also had the experience of taking care of patients with unpredictable aggressive behavior. The charge nurse's prime concern, above my father's care, was to ensure the safety of her staff. Understanding this situation did not make it easier for me. It actually made it more difficult. So far, in my early nursing career, I had not experienced any love for the hostile patients I had cared for. In fact, I often felt relieved when they were transferred to another unit. I was not feeling any relief with this decision about my father and was not concerned about how the nurses carrying for my father were feeling.

My mother had difficulty grasping the severity of this situation. My brother and I explained that transferring my father was for the best—this new facility would be better equipped to manage the care he needed. She nodded silently.

The ambulance attendants arrived soon afterwards and strapped my semi-conscious father onto the stretcher. They secured three sets of straps: one around his chest, pinning his arms by his side; one across his abdomen to hold him on the stretcher; and another around his lower legs. My father was not going anywhere.

Standing to the side, my mind flashed to a memory from *Silence of the Lambs* when the prison guards strapped Hannibal Lecter onto a stretcher. I was watching my father with two sets of eyes: the eyes of a nurse, well aware of what needed to take place to manage an aggressive patient; and the eyes of a daughter who could not believe her father's life was ending like this.

The nurse gave the paramedics a verbal report as well as written instructions to take with them. I wanted nothing more than to add my own testimony about what a great man my father was and how he would never knowingly be physically aggressive with another innocent human being. I wanted to tell them how hard he had always worked, to make sure that his family was provided for. I wanted to tell them, "Don't judge my father by what you see right now."

But I didn't say anything. I kept my emotions and my thoughts to myself. Expressing myself would not change how they had to handle an out-of-control patient. Besides, I knew I'd only get empathetic nods from the crew as they moved a little quicker out of the uncomfortable situation that my defensive thoughts about my father could have created. My family and I thanked the staff members of the nursing home for the care and attention they had given all of us. They sent us on our way with some teary good wishes and hugs. We got into our vehicles, carrying my father's few meager belongings, and headed toward the next step of our family's journey.

I thought we had felt heartbreak standing in the nursing home's environment, but nothing prepared us for where they next sent my father. This unit's atmosphere was filled with fear, anger, and hopelessness from the patients and their family members. We could hear moaning and yelling. We watched a naked patient run away from two staff members attempting to restrain him. My father had already arrived and was sitting in a reclining chair in his room. A restraining jacket, tied at the back of his chair, was securely in place to ensure he would not be able to move. His dentures had been removed, no doubt for safety.

Our family witnessed my father becoming thinner and weaker as his weight dropped over the next week. He was still refusing to eat. Nurses provided some jelled water, a thickened source of liquid to prevent choking, hoping he would swallow even a tiny amount. Our family's encouragement resulted in him taking only a couple of sips. His lips became cracked and dry. The skin on his body began to hang loosely over his bones. Once round and full, his face looked gaunt. I only recognized his prominent nose. He looked like someone had vacuumed all the fat cells out of his body, leaving only a translucent layer of skin stretched over bones. I was happy to have inherited my father's deep blue eyes. Now a pair of pale, milky grey orbits just stared at me. I wondered if Dad's lack of nourishment had changed his eye color or if the change resulted from the lack of life left in his eyes.

While growing up, I sometimes watched my dad prepare for the day. He took pride in his appearance and after applying a dab of Brylcreem in his hands, he would rub them together, quickly moving his hands around in his hair. He spread the cream throughout. Then after combing his hair back, Dad would use his comb to create a neat part on the left. Once the part was in place, he took both hands and squeezed his hair between them to create a wave. I had never known my father not to have his signature wave. Now his hair was thin, dry, and disordered. The nursing staff only had time to keep a patient clean—styling hair was not a priority or one of their duties. At this point, it didn't matter. We were now spending time with only a shadow of the man he once was. A wave in his hair would make no difference.

On March 23, 2004, I was sitting in the unit's lounge area beside my dad, his head drooped. Other patients, also restrained in their chairs, surrounded us. I recognized one of the physicians I had worked with years ago. This amazingly brilliant man, admired by his peers for the breakthroughs he had discovered in medicine, was not doing his daily rounds. Instead, he was sitting at the table with my father. This skillful doctor was also restrained and unaware of where or who he was. I felt a connection to my father's feeling of hopelessness, and I leaned over and whispered into his ear. "This is no way to live, is it, Dad?"

He looked up at me with a sad expression and shook his head, "No."

"It's okay to let go," I told him. "We will take care of Mom." He dropped his head once more and did not respond. Two days later, in the early hours of the morning, after all his children and grandchildren spent a little time with him, and while my mother held his hand, my father left this world.

The doctor caring for my dad had written a liberal order for morphine. The nurses administered it every two hours before they repositioned my father. I knew his breathing had become calmer, and the periods of apnea in between breaths had become longer. The morphine was supporting his transition with ease. Even though he was showing all the signs of being comfortable, I still nodded yes to the nurse when she asked if I wanted my father to have more morphine. I wanted to ensure my father was comfortable and to protect what little endurance and reserve my mother had left.

It was difficult for our family to witness the mental and physical decline in our loving patriarch. He had taught us, by example, how to live a life filled with integrity, honesty, and powerful work ethics. We were proud of him, and even though we would miss him, we were grateful he had found peace.

I know my father felt hopeless and depressed at the end of his life—unable to figure out what was happening and why. All he needed was permission to let go.

I kept thinking, "Why did he have to experience this difficult journey to his death? What lesson was there for him to learn?"

In time, I learned the lesson was not his alone, but mine as well.

Having experienced my father's passage through the end of his life, I became a more understanding, empathetic nurse. Now when I meet my patients, I have a choice: see them as one of many patients on a journey with their illness, or see them as individuals whose experience is one of a kind. Viewing each person as a unique human being helps me remember that the person I am caring for could be my brother, my mother, or even myself. Because of my father, I now interact with my patients in an individualized, personal, and compassionate way.

QUESTIONS TO ASK YOURSELF

1. As a nurse caring for patients with dementia, what feelings do you have about their behavior?

2. What can you say or do to make a violent situation safe for your patient as well as you yourself?

3. What support could you give the families of patients with dementia?

CHAPTER 2

CARING FOR NURSES FACING DEATH

Be prepared for him who knows how to ask questions.
There is one who remembers the way to your door:
Life you may evade, but Death you shall not.

—*T.S. Eliot*

AFTER READING THIS CHAPTER

You will recognize that past life experiences can influence coping strategies.

You will be sensitive to patients' verbal and nonverbal communication.

THE DESOLATE DECISION - SUICIDE

June was 26 years old when she died by suicide. She left behind a two-year-old son, boyfriend, family, and friends in shock and disbelief. My dear friend and I had connected when we were working together as licensed practical nurses. We often said how perfect it was for us to work with a good friend.

June's vitality when working impressed me. Caring for a baby as a single mom and providing care for patients on a palliative unit could be taxing. This 5'4" spark of energy would be among the first to jump up and answer a patient's call bell. The rest of us would still be registering which room bell rang when June would already be walking briskly down the hallway.

When her little boy was two, June moved to Vancouver with her son and new boyfriend to begin a wonderful life with her little family. When she called me, I could hear how excited and happy she was about her new home and the health care position she found that allowed her to spend many hours with her son. Even though I missed our time together, I was very happy for her.

Unfortunately, three months after they moved, June's results from a recent pap smear came back positive for malignant cells. Her doctors were optimistic that with surgery and radiation, she would be cancer free and live a long life. June appeared confident about her consultation with the oncologist and never shared any fears or doubts with others or me. She and her boyfriend discussed their best options. They both realized that the support June required would be best provided back home. Family and friends could care for her and June's son while she underwent treatments. She planned to move back to Alberta and end the live-in relationship with her boyfriend for now.

In hindsight, June showed signs that she had plans other than returning home. The night before she was supposed to leave, June changed her routine. Instead of doing the supper dishes and making lunches while her boyfriend bathed and prepared June's son for bed, she bathed him herself, tucked him into bed, and read him a story. Then when friends stopped by for the evening, June played her guitar and sang sad songs filled with regret and longing for a different life. Eventually, June and her boyfriend went to bed. That night, for the first time, June initiated lovemaking. In the morning, he woke up next to her cold body. June had overdosed on a pain medication left over from an old injury.

Her boyfriend found letters she had written to him and her son on the bedside table. In the letters, she asked for their forgiveness and understanding. She told them she could not imagine her life ending with declining health and having to depend on others for her care. She could not visualize her death being anything but filled with pain and fear. She had witnessed many disturbing deaths during her medical career, and had nightmares about her life ending this way, even though her doctor had assured he was optimistic about June's response to treatment.

June had kept the memories of nursing patients at the end stages of their lives. She could not imagine being on the same journey herself. She saw only one choice—take control. She wanted to plan her own death rather than permit the disease process to dictate how and when she would die.

As friends and colleagues, we felt guilt, sadness, anger, and frustration after she passed. We were close to her. Could we have noticed these changes in her behavior prior to her suicide?

"If only she had been able to express those fears, we would have helped her work through them," we said, placing the responsibility on June.

It did not take long for us to realize that June wouldn't have reached out with her true feelings and doubts, given her frame of mind. We could have taken the initiative and started the conversation, asking how she was coping with her diagnosis, but we just assumed her confidence and positivity genuinely reflected what she was thinking. Sadly, June was wearing a mask. She had tucked away a life's worth of experience with terminally ill patients in her memory bank, and those experiences emerged full force when she was faced with her own mortality.

To prevent tragic events like June's death, we caregivers are now encouraged to share our experiences and emotions about our patients after they have died. Today, if a death occurs that is exceptionally difficult to cope with, medical staff have access to counselors, many of whom cared for the patient who died, so a nurse who requests counseling already feels connected in some way to the counselor. As medical staff, we develop connections with our patients and their families. More challenging or prolonged death often deepens these relationships. I'm not certain how firmly June's "I'm fine and coping" mask was in place, or had there had been counseling available, whether she would have attended a meeting. What I am certain of is that the conversations June and I had would be different now. Hindsight is always perfect vision.

As a nurse, I want not only to take care of my patients' needs but also to ensure that my peers are cared for. Medical caregivers take care not only of patients; they also need to care for each other. Sharing with our loved ones at home what we have witnessed during a stressful day can leave them feeling at a loss about how to best support us. Nevertheless, nurses know what we all go through, so we can be powerful support for each other, if we create those opportunities.

Supporting your peers can be as easy as sharing coffee and a conversation. Recognizing fatigue, frustration, or a fading personality can signal that your colleague is not as resilient as she usually seems. Reaching out to give support can work both ways. You could say, "I noticed that you seem frustrated when you got your assignment this morning" or, "Is everything all right?" or, "I care about you. Do you want to talk?" In this way, we not only become a support, but we also become supported.

Often my colleagues and I would go for breakfast after a particularly stressful night shift, giving us an opportunity to share and de-stress together. Going home after one of our breakfasts always had me feel connected, understood, and more relieved from my concerns.

June's funeral was very elaborate. The front of the church was over flowing with flowers. I will never forget the cluster of carnations in the shape of a large guitar positioned upright on top of her casket. The ribbon wrapped around the unique arrangement read, "Always loved." The minister's words remain with me. "What if June had received these flowers while she was still alive?"

I am not sure flowers would have made a difference, but unconditional love and providing a safe environment for June to share her troublesome thoughts might have given her the support she needed to deal powerfully with cancer. We best serve our patients, each other, and ourselves by being aware that our own experiences and beliefs play a big part in how we cope with death.

QUESTIONS TO ASK YOURSELF

1. After a particularly difficult day, how do you relieve your stress?

2. If you need to speak to someone about feeling sad or overwhelmed, who could you have this conversation with? What do you say to peers you think are having a difficult time?

3. Does the unit you work on have a system in place to support you if you need it?

FINAL ACCEPTANCE

Marilyn was a nurse. Her admission onto our unit came shortly after her diagnosis of leukemia requiring a bone marrow transplant. In her 40s, she was having difficulty coping with her diagnosis and the treatment she needed to survive. When I say she was having difficulty coping, I mean she was difficult to get along with. On our unit, every patient had a designated primary nurse assigned. When that nurse was on duty, she cared for her patient. The problem was no one wanted to be Marilyn's primary nurse.

I am not sure how or why I volunteered, but I did, and our journey together began. I saw Marilyn as someone who had met Death face-to-face and was very afraid. I could understand why she demanded things and was unpleasant at times. She was fighting for her life the only way she knew how: be in control. When I allowed Marilyn to say what she wanted and needed, she began to trust me. Slowly she opened up, and we were able to address some of her fears. This allowed her to move through her treatment more easily and confidently.

I would often walk into her room and find her sitting in a chair, looking out of the window deep in thought. I didn't ask her directly what she was thinking, but I would say, "You appear to be deep in thought." Just sharing this observation gave Marilyn the opportunity to share if she wanted—or not. Over time, Marilyn told how much she loved her career in nursing and her concern that she might never be able to work again. She felt jilted from her planned future, fearing she would also lose the relationship she had with her husband. He was unsure how to support her; she was just as unsure about how to ask for his support.

Unfortunately, Marilyn did not have a positive response to her treatment. The care that she was to receive now would have her on a different path, a path on which all her fears became reality. Almost overnight, she became more withdrawn and less communicative. There was no spark left. She no longer cared enough to be difficult. She had emotionally removed herself from her own life. At her request, a "No Visitors" sign hung on her door. She no longer cared to see family or friends. Her husband was the only one she wanted to see. Unfortunately, he was already struggling before her change of condition, wondering how he could best support his wife. Now he was finding her prognosis even more difficult to cope with. He spent less and less time visiting, finding it easier to call the unit for a progress report. His absence added another level of despair to Marilyn's state of mind.

We always offered counseling to each of our patients through the psychosocial department in our hospital. Marilyn refused to have counselors come into her room. Every day I could see she had less of a desire to do anything or to talk. She was giving up hope. I told her about the benefits of speaking to someone who had the training and the tools to support her.

"They have never gone through this, so how could they know?"

At that moment, I experienced a deeper connection with Marilyn's experience. Her words echoed the ones I had said myself when my baby was born still, and I traveled my own journey of despair. Somehow, I needed to make a connection with Marilyn during her grief.

I sat down beside her, took her hand, and told her I could not imagine nor pretend to know what she was going through. Besides my nursing tasks, I knew the most powerful thing I had to offer was my care and support.

"I'm here for you, Marilyn. You can count on me."

Over the next few days, I saw Marilyn move from despair to what appeared to be acceptance. I observed even a physical change in her. She looked more peaceful and relaxed. On my last night shift about two weeks later, the night was unusually quiet. I told my colleagues that I was taking my break in Marilyn's room. By this time, she was moving in and out of some deep, long periods of unconsciousness. Occasionally she opened her eyes and looked at me. I would smile and go back to my letter writing. When she whispered, "What are you doing?" it was difficult for her to hear, so I moved my chair closer to her.

"I'm writing to a girlfriend in Scotland. We worked as nurses together. We didn't even like each other at first. She ended up being my bridesmaid!"

I laughed when I told Marilyn this story. She managed to smile. When I finished talking, Marilyn looked at me and said, "I love you, Meina."

"Wow," I thought to myself. "It didn't matter that I didn't have words of wisdom and all the answers to make her death easier. Just my being here—connecting and caring—is all she needs."

I told Marilyn, "I love you, too."

She died the next day.

I found it easier to understand Marilyn's response to what she was experiencing because I could relate to her through my own experience with loss. Marilyn arrived at our unit angry. She wasn't upset with anyone in particular. She just had no control over her life. She had no control over what was happening to it.

Here was a woman who had taken up nursing as her vocation. That little girl's dream of being a nurse had become a reality. Marilyn had been the one in charge of her patients' care. She dealt quickly and efficiently with decisions regarding their medical care. Then, in a heartbeat, Marilyn's role changed. When wearing her professional nursing uniform, she showed the world her accomplishment and power. In the hospital as a patient her vocation, like her uniform, was stripped off and replaced with a drab, washed-out gown. In these new combat fatigues, she lost her individuality as soon as she walked through our unit's door. Not only did she lose her identity, she also lost her right to be in control of her treatments. Of course, she could choose whether to have treatments or not, but signing the consent forms gave us permission to take over managing her care, and essentially, managing her life.

Our nursing unit had protocols and procedures to ensure we delivered care smoothly and optimally. Marilyn became part of that flow. Her new experience of being a patient and the uncertainty of her future led her from anger, to withdrawal, and then back again. Like a pendulum, Marilyn's mood changed frequently as she reacted to the external forces around her.

When the nurse coming in at 4:00 a.m. to draw blood and take Marilyn's vital signs woke Marilyn out of a sound sleep, she could be calm or irritable, depending on the nurse's approach. A nurse who was sleep deprived and counting the minutes until she could crawl into her own bed might subconsciously switch on an overhead light without warning, appearing to be thoughtless or uncaring. The doctor who rushed in too quickly to do his daily assessment, promising to come back to answer her questions later, had Marilyn go from feeling cared about to frustrated and forgotten in a matter of moments.

When Marilyn died, I believe she experienced some degree of peace, but I also sensed she felt more resignation than acceptance. Much like June, Marilyn felt disempowered when Death came knocking.

QUESTIONS TO ASK YOURSELF

1. If your assignment included a difficult patient, how could you connect with him or her?

2. What could you say that would validate his or her feelings?

3. No matter what you do or say, your patient still exhibits anger and frustration. How do you usually react to anger or frustration? How else could you react?

BEING EMPOWERED IN THE FACE OF DEATH

I worked with Peg on two of our night shifts every two weeks. We had been on the same schedule for more than a year. Peg was a wonderful, committed, caring nurse and a loving mother of two little boys.

Five of us worked on night shift together, and we had all noticed that Peg was looking fatigued, struggling to stay awake. Peg didn't appear too concerned and blamed her exhaustion on trying to sleep for an hour or two a day while her little ones napped. I could not imagine functioning on this little amount of sleep during the day and having to return to work that next night. During our night shift, we each had an hour break. Many of us took a nap in the nursing lounge during that hour. Our fellow nurses would call us at the end of the break in case our nap became a deep sleep, which it often did.

Peg was the only one who did not have the luxury of going home to bed and sleeping for a solid eight hours before returning to work. Through witnessing her struggle with fatigue, we realized how fortunate we were that our children were grown and that we did not have to sacrifice our sleep in order to take care of our children. We supported Peg by giving up our break time, picking up her workload, and allowing her to sleep an extra hour or two. It gratified us to see that she looked more rested when she woke up after her break.

However, in the next couple of months, Peg grew more fatigued. We felt concerned when she called in sick for her two night shifts. The following week we learned why. Shocked, stunned, and shaken, we listened to our head nurse tell us that Peg would not be returning to work. She had been diagnosed with leukemia and would be admitted to our unit for treatment. We would now be taking care of one of our own.

Almost every nurse asked to be Peg's primary nurse. Everyone Peg worked with loved her. Caring for her would be no different from caring for a family member. Given her poor response to treatment, the oncologists did not expect a positive outcome. Soon, Peg was receiving palliative care to support her living the rest of her life in comfort and peace. Doctors discharged Peg so she could go home and plan for the care of her children. She interviewed many nannies to find the perfect one she could trust to provide loving, comforting support after she was gone. Peg went to her children's school, sharing with the teachers what the future would be like, and enlisting them in the support she wanted for her sons.

Peg put her life in order. She made sure that documents like her children's immunization records and birth certificates were easily accessible. She spent time writing personal letters. As friends and coworkers, we were in awe of the inner strength she had to move powerfully forward. Her greatest wish was to die before December. She did not want her children to have the Christmas month be a reminder of her death. She wanted her children to experience fun and excitement during such a special holiday.

When she had everything arranged, Peg told her husband she was ready to go to the hospital. Arriving on our unit for the last time, Peg greeted her colleagues with a grateful smile. She knew she was in the perfect place to get the best supportive care possible.

This is when I confronted my own weakness. I could not bring myself to enter Peg's room and spend time with her. She represented my deepest personal fear—dying and leaving my children behind. What could I say to her? The words of comfort that I gave so easily to other patients would not be enough. It was easier to remain silent and removed. Thoughts and emotions of losing my son surfaced. Even though his loss was not related to Peg's situation, I still struggled. I did not trust myself. I was afraid I would dissolve into tears in front of her. I chose to stay away and protect myself.

My self-preservation added a layer of guilt after Peg died. During Peg's memorial service, I could not stop crying—not only for her, but also for the remorse I felt for not having said "goodbye." I was left feeling incomplete. I had worked with this amazing person for more than a year. I would not be able to tell her what a remarkable nurse she had been and how I respected everything she had done for our patients. The opportunity to express my admiration to her directly was gone.

When I think of Peg now, I am still in awe of what it must have taken her to accomplish all she did before she died. Many of my patients live in shock and denial to the very end. They move toward death like walking through quicksand, every day slowly deteriorating and dying in anger, regret, and sadness. Their death occurs long before they stop breathing.

In contrast, Peg empowered not only her life, but also the lives of those whom she loved. She gifted me with the insight to look at my own fears and to trust my feelings and knowledge. After Peg's death, I realized it was not always necessary to find the perfect words. Over time, I have given myself permission to move beyond my guilt about not being there for her. I did not need to be a source of strength for Peg; she had her own.

QUESTIONS TO ASK YOURSELF

1. How would you react if someone you knew was admitted to your unit with a terminal diagnosis?

2. What could you say to support her or him?

3. Where and how would you get your own support?

CHAPTER 3

DEALING WITH DIFFICULT PATIENTS

We are not discouraged.
Even though our outer nature suffers decay,
our inner self is renewed day after day.

2 Corinthians 4:16

AFTER READING THIS CHAPTER

You will record interactions with your patients professionally and thoroughly.

You will formulate the best connection with your patient possible, regardless of your patient's response, which will empower you.

THE MANIPULATIVE PATIENT

Even though our nursing staff received a report before James' admission, we were still unprepared. He was our first, a prisoner charged with murder.

He shuffled up to the desk, his hands secured with a set of handcuffs in front of his waist, locked onto a chain that dropped down to his shackled ankles. Two hefty guards escorted him, one on each side. James was going nowhere on his own.

While in the remand centre, waiting for trial, James had become ill with symptoms of abdominal pain and a general malaise. Blood tests, abdominal x-rays, and finally a CT of the abdomen revealed an aggressive abdominal lymphoma.

One of our nurses led the way, and the resounding jingling of the chains echoed throughout the hallways. Visitors and other patients watched James shuffle to the room reserved for him. His room was at the end of the corridor, separated as much as possible from the rest of the unit's activities. Our nursing staff nervously looked at each other. Taking care of criminals was an area of nursing we had learned nothing about in our textbooks.

During a preadmission conference, our Unit Manager determined that James would not have a primary nurse. An earlier description and report from the remand centre had told us that he could be manipulative and cunning. Our charge nurse decided that our best plan was to limit regular contact with him. Despite having these safeguards in place, it was not long before James had figured out nurses' rotations. He would ask why he had not seen a certain nurse.

"Isn't she working now?" he would ask.

After hearing these types of questions, nurses traded shifts to put another level of precaution into place.

Senior nurses felt more capable of caring for the man. We kept younger and new graduate nurses assigned to our other patients. Even though they were not in direct contact with James, they still listened and learned from the reports at the end of our shift as we updated the oncoming staff members.

James was with us for a few months. During this time, he could be pleasant when it served his motives. If he wanted something—like another round of dessert—butter could melt in his mouth the way he asked us for it. His request usually ended with one of his dazzling smiles. We found it easy to cope with his smooth-talking demeanor. When he acted this way, we felt relatively at ease. However, nothing prepared us for the violent rages that would sometimes consume him. His cursing would echo down the hallway. We understood that it was best not to respond to these rants. Instead, we would leave the room and return later to finish our duties when he was calmer.

James' feet were shackled to the end of his bed. A prison guard sat outside the door twenty-four hours a day, but these safety measures gave us caregivers a false sense of security. The guard would reprimand James for his angry outbursts, but James usually met these reprimands with more profanity directed toward the guard. The guard's only power over his prisoner was ensuring that James' shackles remained in place.

James could be polite, angry, submissive, or cruel. We never knew which way he would be when we entered his room. At the beginning of our shift, we received a report from the nurse going off duty. However, James' mood with the previous nurse was not necessarily the same mood that he'd exhibit when we entered his room for the first time during the new shift.

I found his cruel mood the most difficult to deal with. He seemed to have a sixth sense for knowing a person's most vulnerable areas, zeroing in on them by saying hurtful things. For me, he targeted my weight. I was drawing his blood from his central line one morning when he said sweetly, "Can I ask you something?"

I looked up at him, and we locked eyes. I was shocked how dark and cold his eyes were. I could not even discern his pupil from the rest of his eye. It was like looking into a black lagoon.

"Yes, you can ask me," I told him.

"Are you pregnant, or do you just look like a cow?"

I felt cold, numb, and paralyzed by his question. It took every effort to control my shock and anger. I wanted so badly to say, "You're pretty

*%@+#ing brave saying something like that when I could so easily inject a syringe of air into your central line!"

I also knew that any response to put James in his place would have only fed his little sport. I met his gaze with a cool indifference, saying nothing in response, refusing to be a pawn in his little mind game. Finishing my task, I gathered my supplies and was surprised that my hands were not shaking. I wondered if he could hear the hammering of my heart. I purposefully opened up the curtains to show I was in no hurry to leave his room. Walking down the hall toward the nursing desk, I began to shake. By the time I reached the desk, I burst into tears, feeling hurt and humiliated. With the support of my colleagues, I realized that I had responded just as he had wanted, only not in front of him. I also knew I had to continue my shift with him. It would have been easy for me to have another nurse continue his care and for me to retreat to a safer environment. However, I was determined that he would not get under my skin. Later, I returned to his room with what I hoped was a detachment to his previous comments. He had had his fun with me. The remainder of that shift was uneventful. I felt relieved and proud of myself for fulfilling my duties as his nurse. I discovered the depth of my own maturity and courage that evening.

Caring for people with a history like James led me to reflect on the fairness of life. Why do many young, innocent people die, while someone who has committed murder is given the chance for a cure? It would be so easy for me to become self-righteous about my feelings. I realize this moral dilemma is not mine to solve. I was hired to do a job and do it with integrity. There would be no room to play the devil's advocate in these situations. I could, though, play my own game and that would be giving the best of what I have to give to those who need it, regardless of their actions or words.

I could see James was experiencing fear and anger. As he went through his own coping stages with a potentially terminal illness, he was no different from other patients. When I made this connection, it was easier to put my own feelings aside about him.

After treatment, James' tests confirmed that he was in remission and possibly cured from his cancer. He was discharged and escorted back to prison. A month later, we read in the newspaper that the courts released him from jail due to a technicality discovered during his hearing. I can only hope that when Death stopped knocking on James' door, he found a new, empowering way to live his life.

QUESTIONS TO ASK YOURSELF

1. If your assignment included a prisoner, how could you connect with her/him?

2. What would your response have been if James had personally attacked you with a hurtful comment?

3. Look at your own thoughts around fairness and can you separate your views when giving care?

THE ANGRY PATIENT

Mr. V. was a different kind of "difficult" patient. I watched as he stood up from the waiting room when I called his name. It was obviously frustrating for him to be at the cancer center. I recognized the signs of anger and realized that underneath his anger was probably fear. When I called his name, his wife stood up to answer. She nudged him to stand, so he slowly got up. As they moved toward me, he avoided eye contact and kept his focus on anything but me. He let out a loud sigh as I showed them the examination room and invited them to enter. I followed them and introduced myself.

Mr. V. was having five radiation treatments for a metastatic lung cancer. His treatments were not for a cure. They were for controlling the side effect of hemoptysis he was experiencing. Hemoptysis is coughing up blood, which might occur when patients have lung cancer. The radiation treatments often prescribed in these situations are to minimize these side effects.

His wife chose to sit in a chair close to me. Mr. V. stood with his arms crossed. I invited him to sit in one of the other available chairs. He picked the one closest to the door. Not only did he keep his arms crossed, he also crossed his legs. Though these were physical, non-verbal signs, I could tell he was protecting himself from a possible threat by being defensive.

Mrs. V. leaned forward toward me, rushing to tell me about her husband's breathing.

"He's increasingly short of breath when he exerts himself, and he coughs up green-colored sputum."

"Does he have a fever?" I asked.

"He'd had some chills for the last couple of days."

Mr. V. looked like he was not even listening. I rolled my chair closer to him, to ask if he had felt a change in his breathing.

"No," he grunted.

Then he stood up, started pacing the floor, and moved toward the door. His wife let out an exasperated sigh as she stood up to join her husband. He could not wait until he got out of the room. Obviously, she would be going with him. Even though they were no longer looking at me, I explained that I wanted to listen to Mr. V.'s lungs.

"My lungs are fine," he said abruptly. "I just want to go home. I have a long drive ahead of me."

As they were opening the door to leave, I walked toward them, saying, "I am really concerned that there may be an infection. Could I at least take your temperature?"

I thought getting his temperature would give me information I could use to keep him there. However, he shook his head no and moved into the hallway.

Again, I tried. "It's Friday. With the weekend coming up, I want to make sure you are okay before you leave here."

Mr. V. had his back to me. I saw him put his hand in the air, motioning with one brisk wave that he was not interested. His wife slowly followed him into the hallway, shaking her head and muttering something about her husband being stubborn.

I followed them a few yards to the elevator and tried once more. "Please make sure you see a doctor or the emergency department if your symptoms do not improve."

The elevator came, and they both got on silently. Mr. V. did not respond or make eye contact. His wife nodded her head slowly toward me, indicating she would do what she could. Then the elevator door closed.

After I saw Mr. V. and his wife, my charting was not as detailed as it could have been. The progress note page had limited writing space, and I had many other patients waiting. I wrote, "Pt. had chills, a productive cough, but was in a hurry to leave." I omitted the part about my concern and that I had wanted to do a further assessment on him, but that he refused. I also omitted the fact that the conversation took place by the elevator where I encouraged them to seek medical attention if his symptoms persisted.

This experience taught me the importance of fully charting events as they happened. The extra time it would have taken me to get another piece of paper, place Mr. V.'s patient label on it, and continue the charting would have saved me time and frustration in the end.

Two days after I had seen Mr. V., he died of double pneumonia. His radiation doctor received notice from the College of Physicians informing him of his patient's death a month later. Mr. V.'s wife was charging negligence for lack of assessment done at our center. She stated that she felt her husband would not have died had we taken more time to examine him. She said she had also expressed her concern that a nurse only saw him. She claimed a physician should have been called.

Thankfully, I had written enough of an entry that I could not be faulted. Our practice was to call a physician if we had a concern, but this patient had not wanted to wait, even for a simple temperature check, let alone a chest x-ray.

Obviously, not all patients are compliant and cooperative. The circumstances they are facing are new and frightening to them. Their emotions come from deep within. Many do not even know how to relate to how they are feeling, let alone convey these symptoms to nurses and doctors. Some are in denial about their diagnosis. When they exhibit new symptoms, those just add more proof about their disease, leaving them feeling confronted with more than they can cope with.

In hindsight, I probably could not have done things differently with Mr. V., other than enter more detailed notes. Perhaps I could have expressed my concerns to the patient's physician and asked him to call the patient at home. Realistically, though, physicians depend on their nurses to assess patients and communicate their concerns. That is what nurses are trained to do. If physicians were to call every patient who refused to have their current vital signs assessed, there would be little time left to evaluate patients who need and want to be seen.

I trust that Mrs. V eventually got closure with her husband's death. Placing blame on a faceless institution is not unusual, but can make the grief process longer. When a nurse made a standard follow-up phone call to Mrs. V to find out how she was managing, she just hung up.

QUESTIONS TO ASK YOURSELF

1. What would you say to a patient you were concerned about who does not want to be assessed?

2. After hearing your patient had died like Mr. V., what might you be feeling?

3. How could you comfortably take the time you need for charting, knowing many others waited to see you?

CHAPTER 4

FAITH IN THE FACE OF DEATH

Everybody wants to go to Heaven,
but no one wants to die.

—*Loretta Lynn*

AFTER READING THIS CHAPTER

You will be empowered to respect your patients' religious beliefs and practices.

You will evaluate your own thoughts and reactions when caring for a patient with a belief system different from your own.

QUESTIONING FAITH

My mother told me about Mr. B., a devout Christian who rarely missed a Sunday church service. However, my mother said he never had a deep personal discussion about God or his beliefs with his fellow parishioners or family. Any thoughts he had or questions about his convictions remained unspoken. He focused on attending church and the rituals that went along with it. No room existed for doubt or expansion on anything he already had learned.

During a visit with my mom, a few years before Mr. B's death, he shared with her that he was not "sure" about what would happen to him after he died. He also admitted he was skeptical about some stories in the Bible.

"I read my Bible daily looking for answers," he said. "But I can't find clear answers to my questions."

"Maybe you should speak to your minister about your questions," my mother suggested.

"I could do that, but I should know this myself."

Although my mother did not know for sure, she told me she doubted that he ever had a conversation with his minister to get any deeper insight or clarification.

Mr. B. lived an average life with his wife, and they raised a family of five children. When the children were younger, they all committed to their church, attending services twice on Sunday—once in the morning and again in the evening. In between services, the family remained in their Sunday clothes. Physical activity was forbidden. The children could not ride their bikes or play ball. They could only sit quietly reading a book. They read a Bible verse and gave a prayer of thanks before eating a meal, whether at home or in a restaurant. Ironically, Mr. B., the head of the household, appeared to be living a self-disciplined life—at peace with his religious beliefs. On the inside, though, he felt uncertain. Doubt nagged him.

Mr. B's inner conflict bothered him not only spiritually, but he was also estranged from one of his sons, who was gay. The father and son no longer spoke to each other. For Mr. B, being gay violated all the principles and beliefs he was raised to adhere to. The son had moved away, making it easier not to attend family functions where he might be uncomfortable. For several years, Mr. B. either did not speak to his son or limited the conversations to superficial chats. Before his passing, Mr. B.'s diminished hearing made it very difficult to have a telephone conversation, even with the assistance of a hearing aid.

Their son would call and speak to his mother and have her pass on a greeting to his father. When he realized his father was aging and his health was declining, the need to reconcile with his father became more urgent. The son wanted nothing more than to have his father understand that he did not choose to be gay. The other children in the family, although understanding their brother's need to get closure with their father, were fearful that this type of conversation would have consequences. Mr. B. was frail and spending more time immobile. Everyone was protecting Mr. B from hearing a conversation that might be a risk to his health. His son's unspoken words were to remain unheard.

As a nurse, you might find yourself entrusted with the innermost thoughts and secrets of your patients and their families. (According to Gallup polls, year after year the most trusted medical professionals are in nursing.) Family members might sense a need to let go of what had been kept inside, and as medical staff, we could use this as an opportunity to support families by facilitating dialogue between them. Because we have already established a relationship of trust, we can suggest counseling for terminally ill patients, and they may be more likely to act on that advice. For example, if we hear a patient express concern about a child's lifestyle choice, we could ask, "Have you had a conversation with your son about this?" This question could be the opening to suggest that counseling has benefited other families in the past and that you have witnessed the positive healing of relationships.

"We all want nothing but peace in our lives," a nurse might say. "Your son is wishing he could have this with you as well, Mr. B. Would you be willing to speak to someone to give you some tools and suggestions to make this possible?"

Unfortunately, no one ever made the suggestion to Mr. B. He died never having resolved the separation between him and his son. Speaking to Mr. B's son after his father's death, I was happy to hear that he had found his own peace in spite of the rigid stand his father had taken. He understood his father was who he was. Mr. B. would be proud of the forgiving, loving son he raised.

QUESTIONS TO ASK YOURSELF

1. Caring for palliative patients, what could you say to help ensure that they were at peace at the end of their life?

2. If Mr. B. was your patient and you understood that he was estranged from his son, would you feel comfortable suggesting a conversation between them? If not, why not?

3. What support could you offer to Mr. B's son if you were aware of the separation between him and his father?

UNWAVERING FAITH

As medical staff, we might also find ourselves having difficulty empathizing with our patients because of their belief patterns or faith. Ellie, a 20-year-old Jehovah's Witness, realized the risks that she would be taking when admitted for an autologous stem cell transplant for her Acute Myeloid Leukemia.

Ellie said she was aware of the treatment regime and the side effects of the high dose chemotherapy she needed before her transplant. Her physician emphasized the probability of needing the support of red blood cells and platelets.

"I'm concerned that your religion does not favor blood transfusions," he said.

"My faith is strong," Ellie replied. "I feel supported by a higher power, and I trust that I will not need a transfusion of blood."

Admission day arrived. Accompanied by her parents, Ellie presented herself to our unit. Her primary nurses escorted her to a private room, which would be hers for the next two months. While filling out her admission forms, Ellie told her nurse, "I'm a Jehovah's Witness. Is your staff aware of this?"

Our unit's medical staff was well aware of Ellie's religious beliefs, as well as what potentially lay ahead for this young girl. Among ourselves, we discussed our inability to understand why Ellie and her family would agree to an aggressive stem cell transplant treatment but refuse necessary blood transfusions. We agreed that it would have been better for Ellie to have no treatments than to spend the little amount of life she had left coping with the harsh side effects of a transplant. Of course, nothing we could do or say would reverse Ellie's strong conviction.

The attending physician suggested an injection of G-CSF as a means to boost her blood counts, but she declined the offer. G-CSF is not a blood product, so we were surprised at her unwavering decision.

I watched Ellie and her parents smile at each other as the doctor left the room. It was as though the three family members shared a special secret that the medical personnel were not privy to. My colleagues and I believed that to exercise faith and trust in a difficult or life-threatening situation such as this could give people strength. We often encouraged our patients to use the resources that they have used in the past to get them through a difficult time. This belief system felt different. Ellie and her family were making a choice with faith in their religion, not in our medical system.

We all wondered, "If they had such a strong belief in their religion, why go through this treatment at all? Why not remain home and trust that their belief would cure her leukemia?" At the time, it was beyond my comfort zone to have a conversation with them about their beliefs. Now that I'm older, I feel more comfortable asking patients' questions about their faith and choices. Looking back at Ellie's case, I would now ask her about her faith so I could better understand her beliefs and theories. It would be a learning opportunity for me to develop more compassion and relatedness.

Doctors ordered Ellie's chemotherapy drugs a few days before nurses infused her stem cells through her intravenous access. It did not take long before Ellie's blood counts started to decrease. Nurses drawing her morning blood work would admit to saying silent prayers that the blood count results would be more positive than the ones from the day before. Every patient's room had a large calendar hanging on the wall. When counts of the blood work came in, the primary nurse would write them on the calendar. Physicians, nurses, or other medical personnel entering the room could see these results at a glance. Ellie and her family could see them, too.

As the counts became more critical, the physicians in charge spoke to Ellie, who was experiencing severe side effects with bleeding from her nose and gums, and rectally with each bowel movement. Ellie remained true to her belief. She became too weak to walk to the bathroom, so we placed a commode chair beside her bed. A nurse would assist her to the chair when she needed to use it. In a couple of days, it took two of us to transfer her from the bed to the commode.

When anyone entered her room, a foul smell of blood would assault their senses. If Ellie was aware of it, she never complained. The doctors again had a frank discussion with Ellie and her family, telling them that unless we supported her with a transfusion of red blood cells and platelets, there would be no hope for her to survive. Still the answer was, "No."

Soon, she didn't have enough red blood cells to transport the amount of oxygen she needed to help her breathe. Her respiration became labored, so she had to use an oxygen mask. Her nose filled with dry blood, and she had to breathe through her mouth. Ellie grew weaker. It became impossible to transfer her from the bed to the commode, even with two nurses assisting. She could no longer sit up on her own.

The situation challenged us as nurses changing the sheets and pillowcases, seeing bright red blood ooze from every orifice of this young woman's body onto the crisp white bed linen. If we as caregivers found this upsetting, we silently wondered how her parents were managing to watch their daughter's lifeblood slowly seep from her body. They remained steadfast and diligently sat at her bedside reading passages from the Bible and praying for their daughter. Twelve weeks after her admission to the hospital, Ellie passed away quietly, accepting that there was a bigger "plan" for her than the life she had lived here on earth.

Those of us who cared for Ellie had difficulty accepting the decision that she and her family had made. Many of us had children the same age and could not comprehend remaining committed to a deep religious conviction against a blood transfusion that we knew had the power to save her life. Many patients on our ward were dying and had no choice. We felt very frustrated, even angry, after she died.

Our charge nurse understood the difficult emotions we were experiencing after Ellie's death. She suggested our unit's psychologist come help us cope with this situation. The psychologist encouraged all of us to speak freely about what we were feeling and to share our frustrations about our experience. After hearing other team members express their sadness and helplessness with what they witnessed, we all understood that we were not alone. One nurse began to cry.

"I felt useless and helpless watching Ellie die. I was trained to help my patients regain their health, not to watch them refuse life-saving treatment based on a religious rule."

We left the debriefing feeling validated and knowing that we had done the best we could while still respecting the wishes of our patient. We realized that Ellie had a commitment to her belief system, and she had made a well-informed decision. Our role was not to judge but to support our patients.

QUESTIONS TO ASK YOURSELF

1. If you are caring for a patient who refuses necessary treatment because of religious beliefs, what would you think and how might you feel?

2. Describe several ways you might deal with your own emotions or grief when caring for someone who refuses treatment.

3. What words of comfort could you extend to the family even if you did not agree with their decision?

CHAPTER 5

MAKING DIFFICULT MEDICAL DECISIONS

You never know how strong you are
Until being strong is the only choice you have

—*Bob Marley*

AFTER READING THIS CHAPTER

You will recognize the role of a patient's family throughout the end of his or her life's journey.

You will better able to support and accept challenging circumstances that come up when patients are making health care decisions.

AN UNSPOKEN CHOICE

I remember a patient I called into the examination room to be seen by the Radiation Oncologist and me. This patient looked like Grizzly Adams. His size and appearance made it almost comical to watch him walk beside his sister, who accompanied him to his appointment. She was dressed professionally, complete with briefcase and a smart skirt with matching jacket. I formed the opinion that she must be a corporate lawyer, and when she handed me her business card, I saw that she was. My rough-looking patient, whom I began to affectionately think of as "Grizzly Adams," towered over his sister. He wore hiking boots, a checkered shirt, and suspenders that held up his jeans. Although a large beard covered his face, I got a glimpse of his small, dark brown eyes looking nervously around at his surroundings.

Soon, it became apparent that his sister was taking charge of her brother's consultation with us. She did all the talking while her brother sat quietly beside her, head bent, intently looking down at his boots. Obviously, this man was not going to talk much. He answered our questions in one or two syllable words. He often glanced at the door. I sensed he just wanted to bolt out of the room.

I found out that he lived alone in a cabin he had built 30 years ago in the mountains. His only companion was his faithful dog. A few weeks prior to our meeting, he had experienced a seizure in his yard. His dog had run to the closest neighbor to alert her about his owner's need for help. The neighbor had called my patient's sister. Diagnosed with Stage 4 brain tumor, following surgery he and his sister were now meeting with us to learn more about radiation treatments.

Grizzly Adams' prognosis was grim. The treatments would allow him to live another few months at the most. His sister had moved him to her condominium downtown to support him with rides and care while he underwent treatment. His neighbor was caring for his dog.

After explaining radiation treatments, the physician and I were shocked when our patient spoke.

"Can I go home until I start treatment?" he asked. Since his doctor had no concerns, Grizzly Adams' sister reluctantly agreed to take her brother back to his cabin.

After they left, the physician and I talked about how our patient obviously had no desire for treatments. Earlier, in our discussion with the patient and his sister, the doctor told them it would be reasonable to monitor and use medication for symptom control. Cancelling the radiation treatments was an option. His sister had given her brother little opportunity to express his own thoughts and wishes. The doctor asked him if he understood he would need ten days of treatments. He looked at his sister before nodding yes.

The following Monday morning I received a phone call from his sister. Her brother had died over the weekend. Found on the ground between his cabin and his outside latrine, her brother had transitioned with his beloved dog sitting diligently beside him. The fact that his dog had not run for help this time made me grateful that he was with his master at the end.

I never found out many details about the circumstances of my patient's death or who found him, but I was relieved he had died where he had lived. The thought of this man looking up to the open skies, surrounded by the wilderness he loved as he took his last breath— instead of surrounded by a concrete medical jungle—just felt right to me.

QUESTIONS TO ASK YOURSELF

1. What support could you give a patient when he or she is given the choice of treatment or no treatment?

2. Do you think, in the case of this brother and sister that the patient's wishes were acknowledged? Could anything else have been done to support the patient?

3. What were your thoughts when you heard the patient had died alone?

A DOCTOR'S CHOICE

Thankfully, the days of frowning on nurses being patient advocates are long gone. In the 1970s, nurses were more like doctors' handmaidens who were never supposed to disagree or question a physician's order. Regardless of what we knew, we were not paid to think. We were only supposed to follow doctors' directions.

I worked as a licensed practical nurse on a cancer unit in the 1970s. One day, we admitted a physician's 19-year-old son. He had cancer of the testes that had spread to his lungs, liver, and brain. The admitting physician told our nursing unit staff that under no conditions were we to tell the patient about the severity of his prognosis. These orders came from the young man's father, one of the directors on the hospital board.

Although the young man was very ill, his family had been caring for him at home with nursing care from a community agency. The family had not allowed visitors at the house in several weeks, and they wanted this rule enforced on our unit as well.

We hung a "No Visitors" sign on the patient's door with written instructions to speak to a staff member before entering. The only people visiting this young man were his sister and his parents. To me, it seemed as though he was being held hostage. Too weak to get out of bed, he could not even poke his head outside his door. He spent most of his time alone in his room, aimlessly looking at the television on the wall across from his bed.

Two days after his admission, a young girl appeared at our nursing desk well after visiting hours. She said she was his girlfriend.

"I called his sister," she said, "and found out he was in the hospital now. His sister has been helping me sneak into their house when his parents aren't home. But when I called my boyfriend's parents, they told me again that they wouldn't allow me to see him."

She was crying and pleading for us to let her go in—even for a minute.

Five of us were on duty that evening shift, sitting behind the front desk doing our charting. We looked at each other—all of us thinking the same thing. The nurse in charge was the only one to take action. She got up from behind the desk, took the young girl by the hand, and said, "Come with me." She led the young woman down the hall to her boyfriend's room. The rest of us smiled at each other and pumped invisible arms in the air.

Whenever we came into this young man's room, he never asked many questions. I suspected he knew he was dying. Even though he was not receiving any active cancer treatments, his deteriorating health must have given him clues about his status.

Without fail, his girlfriend continued to sneak up the back stairs into his room at the end of the corridor every evening. She would stay most of the night in the recliner chair we had placed in the room, also making sure she had a comfortable pillow and blanket. The night nurses told the rest of the staff they would often find the two holding each other's hands as they both slept. By the time the day shift arrived at 7:00 a.m., she was long gone. The night nurses always removed any evidence of her having been there.

For the two weeks before he died, his girlfriend came up those stairs and stayed every night. Although only his family members were with him when he died, she had been comforting him every night. I often wondered if his girlfriend and his sister ever broke the father's rule and told the patient his prognosis. I trust that he felt peace at the end.

Before the idea of being a "patient advocate" ever became part of nurses' training, I learned my first powerful lesson about the importance of advocating for a patient from the events and circumstances surrounding this young man's journey with cancer. In his case, we as nurses, were left with a difficult choice: disobey a direct order or refuse the girlfriend's request. We knew in our hearts what would give our patient comfort. Thankfully, that night we had a powerful nurse among us who took the lead. Perhaps she recognized that the orders we had received came from a father's fear, disguised as power and control.

In hindsight, it is easy to imagine how helpless the father must have felt. Years of education and training still did not equip him with enough knowledge and skills to save his own child. The next best thing he could do was to protect his son from any emotional distress that visitors might cause. The only power he had was his position, so he used it.

My second lesson in patient advocacy came not long after this first lesson. Our unit was not as busy as the one below us, so our charge nurse sent another nursing assistant and me down to help. We worked together to complete all the morning care. Then we returned to a young man who was the only patient in a semi-private room. We had been in his room earlier and had noticed a guitar sitting in the corner by his bedside table. He appeared withdrawn; our attempts at conversation were met with monosyllabic answers or a nod of his down cast head.

We thought we would brighten his day with a little song and encourage him to join in. The other nurse picked up the guitar. We sat at the foot of his bed and began to sing. Before long, he joined in. We had not even finished the first stanza before the head nurse briskly marched in and demanded that we come to her office immediately. We both received the rest of the day off without pay. Not only had we broken the cardinal rule of sitting on a patient's bed, but we had also acted unprofessionally by singing while on duty. I thought the lost pay was a small price to pay for brightening this patient's day.

Fortunately, today we focus on patients and what we can do to make them more comfortable. There is no longer a rule against sitting on a patient's bed, although I only do this when I get clear cues from a patient who indicates he or she is open to me moving closer when appropriate. Often, if a terminally ill patient is distressed, I will move my chair closer, reducing the personal space between us. Sometimes I even place my hand on theirs while allowing them to talk. When I sense my patient needs human touch, this also becomes a way for me to reinforce how much I am listening and how much I care. If my intuition is off, and someone pulls his or her hand away, I continue the conversation, allowing my patients to interact with me in a way that they feel comfortable. If a patient cries, I usually offer them a tissue, but I have wondered if this subtle gesture makes them feel that I am telling them to get control and stop crying. To avoid any confusion, when I offer them a tissue now, I say, "This is to help you, not to stop you."

You may never find yourself allowing a girlfriend to sneak into her dying boyfriend's room at night or strumming a guitar while singing at the end of your patient's bed. However, there are many different opportunities for you to connect with your patients, encourage them, and advocate for their needs and wishes (even in seemingly small ways) as they navigate through our challenging healthcare system.

QUESTIONS TO ASK YOURSELF

1. Do you see yourself as a patient advocate? Why or why not?

2. What would you have done if faced with a patient not knowing his or her diagnosis?

3. What conversations could you have with family members who wish to "protect" their loved one from difficult news about their health?

CHAPTER 6

UNFINISHED BUSINESS WITH FAMILY MEMBERS AND FRIENDS

No after, no before.
I hold you close,
I release you to be free;
I am in you and you are in me.

—*Thich Nhat Hanh*

AFTER READING THIS CHAPTER

You will express empathy when relating to a patient's need to find peace.

You will feel confident about your role in supporting your patient and his or her family to find peace.

UNRESOLVED FAMILY ISSUES

Death had been pounding loudly on Mrs. H.'s door for weeks, but she refused to answer. Her physician called our unit requesting a palliative bed because the nursing home where she lived had none available. Later that morning, the ambulance transported Mrs. H. to our unit. When I went to take a report from the paramedics, I thought, "This woman looks like she's ready to deliver a baby." Her abdomen was large and swollen, her skin was yellowish, and her arms looked like two twigs lying outside the blanket. When I said her name, she opened her eyes. When she met my gaze, I saw that dark yellow sclera surrounded her brown eyes. I did not need the paramedic's report to tell me that my new patient's cancer had spread to her liver.

Mrs. H. appeared very close to the end. When I told her my name, she struggled to keep her eyes open, nodding her head slightly in response before she closed them again. I briefly explained to Mrs. H. that we would be moving her into a room and transferring her from the stretcher to a bed. She nodded slightly.

I walked down the hall to her private room while the ambulance crew wheeled the stretcher along behind me. Most of the rooms on our unit offered amazing views of downtown Calgary or the mountains. I knew the views wouldn't matter to Mrs. H. since she would likely be looking only at the bed rails in place for her safety.

Mrs. H's three children, one daughter and two sons, arrived not long after the ambulance left. I was paged to the front desk to meet them. We introduced ourselves, and as we walked down to their mother's room, I orientated them to the unit, emphasizing that they could come and go any time they wished.

The daughter told me that they would be taking turns, and one of them would always be with their mother. To make it more comfortable for them, I told them we could provide a cot for the night if the recliner chair was not sufficient. Our patients appeared to be more peaceful and comfortable when someone was with them. I was glad to hear that Mrs. H. would not be alone.

Her sons went into the room to be with their mother while her daughter remained in the hall outside the door speaking to me. She was obviously the spokesperson for the family, providing me with her phone number as first contact.

"We've all taken time off work now so that we can be with our mother."

She told me that other family had visited and supported their mother in the nursing home. But now that Mrs. H. was in the hospital, the three of them would be the only ones staying with her.

Mrs. H. had been diagnosed with a bowel cancer ten years before. She underwent surgery followed by radiation and chemotherapy treatments. At the time, Mrs. H. was in her seventies. The surgery and treatments had made it difficult for her to care for herself and her home, so she moved to an assisted living center where she stayed until two years ago. During that time, she suffered a small stroke, leaving the right side of her body weak. That was when she moved from the assisted living center to a nursing home.

I felt compassion for this woman who had moved twice in the last two years, not by choice, but by necessity. Now, once again, she had no say about being moved to a hospital. Two months earlier, Mrs. H.'s cancer had metastasized to her liver.

"Just two weeks ago my mother had been enjoying a cup of tea sitting in a chair," said her daughter. "It's so hard to see her declining so quickly." She rapidly blinked back tears.

I did not know what it was like to lose a mother. I still had mine. I had no idea what this family's circumstances and struggles were. Even if I had lost my mother, my experience would not have been the same, and I would still not know exactly what it was like for them. I did however, feel empathy for what they were experiencing.

"It must be hard on all of you," I said.

Then I reassured her that our staff would make her mother's comfort our main priority. I could see that the daughter appeared more relaxed when she heard me say this.

Mrs. H. lingered in and out of consciousness for the next week. Toward the end of the week, the nurses caring for Mrs. H. noticed that, after repositioning her, she would stop breathing for a short period.

Their vigilant stay at their mother's bedside exhausted Mrs. H.'s family. They whispered to us in the hallway, asking, "Does it always take this long?"

We were also surprised that their mother continued to linger on.

"Have you told your mother it's okay to let go?" In my experience, it's often helpful for family members to tell their loved one they will be all right, and that they're free to go.

We learned the children had each told their mother she could go.

As nurses, we are responsible for the care of our patients and their family members. This family's days and nights were long as they balanced their own family's needs with time for their mother. Mrs. H. was their priority, but I could see the struggle being in the hospital with her day after day.

After two days off, I was surprised that Mrs. H. was on my assignment sheet—still with us. I went into the room, and her daughter was just waking up after having spent yet another night beside her mother's bedside. I reintroduced myself and told her that I would be the nurse with them during my shift. I asked her if there had been any change overnight. Her daughter slowly shook her head, "No," and took a deep sigh as she reached into her purse for her cell phone. I could hear her making a call as I was doing some mouth care on Mrs. H. I wiped her face with a warm washcloth and heard her daughter leave someone else a message.

"Lisa, please answer the phone or call us back. We need you here. Mom needs you here."

Then she hung up the phone.

I looked at her inquisitively.

"My youngest sister, Lisa," she said.

"I thought there were only the three children. I don't think I've met Lisa," I said.

As her eyes filled up with tears, she told me, "My mom and Lisa had a falling out years ago. Lisa refuses to see her or speak to her."

Apparently, the family had been calling Lisa frequently, leaving messages and asking her to come see her mother. She responded with silence.

I could now understand why Mrs. H. might be fiercely holding on. She had unfinished business waiting for her daughter to come and say goodbye. I believe no one else could tell Mrs. H. it was okay to let go and all would be well. Only Lisa could do that.

Lisa never came. Mrs. H. died a few days later, never having heard the sound of Lisa's voice.

QUESTIONS TO ASK YOURSELF

1. What words of support could you give to a family if they asked you about how long it might take a person to die?

2. Do you believe an unresponsive patient can still be aware of her surroundings?

3. Would you be able to have a conversation with Mrs. H. even though she did not respond?

LEAVING A MEMORY OF LOVE

Meaghan's mother was on a mission when admitted to our palliative care unit. She was determined to finish knitting a blanket for her daughter, Meaghan, who was five. Given her dire condition, even the inexperienced knitters on our staff could see she had too much knitting still to do to achieve her goal. Spending most of her days in bed, Meaghan's mother was too weak to sit in a recliner for more than an hour at a time. Her unfinished project was always close by her side. She frequently fell asleep having hardly completed a row.

As nurses, we would often pick up the blanket and knitting needles after she had fallen asleep, making sure they were still within reach if she woke up. We knew how important it was to finish this blanket for Meaghan as a memory for her daughter. We often talked around the nurse's charting table about what we could do to support Meaghan's mom. One nurse suggested that she knew how to knit and would be happy to complete the blanket. We all agreed that would not be the same. A third party had no place in the completion of this blanket. This was a labor of love between Meaghan and her mother.

Within a few days, Meaghan's mom passed away. The blanket was unfinished, so I had to pack it up with the rest of her belongings. Meaghan's father was by his wife's bedside when she passed. He had left to go home to tell his little girl her mommy was gone, saying he would pick up his wife's belongings later. Personally, I find it very difficult to pack up patient's personal property after they die. Placing intimate effects into an impersonal hard plastic hospital bag makes me realize how final death is.

I have always taken a little longer to pack up a patient's belongings than the task calls for. Reflecting a moment on each item is almost a spiritual ritual for me. Knowing that the owner will never have an opportunity to touch those belongs again makes their passing absolute. I relate to the loved one who will be unpacking the bag and relate to the emotions that they possibly feel. Unpacking my father's belongings at home after he died was very difficult. What should we do with a pair of glasses that defined how my father looked to me as much as his smile? Years down the road, it was easier to donate his belongings, but at the time, holding his glasses was like holding a part of my father.

I was the one who would transfer these personal items from my former patient's hands to their loved one's hands. The purses of my female patients always move me the most. I could never imagine leaving my house without my purse. It holds everything that I might need. Leaving my purse behind is like leaving part of me behind.

Another nurse and I packed up Meaghan's mom's belongings and put them in a bag. Except for the blanket. We both looked at it and then touched it at the same time.

"I'm so sad for little Meaghan. Her mommy worked so hard to try to finish this," I said.

Both of us were mothers ourselves, and we both had daughters. We empathized deeply with how desperately she wanted to finish this project—a tangible symbol of the love between a mother and her child. Meaghan might never know how desperately hard her mother worked to complete this special gift for her daughter.

My colleague said, "I wonder if the blanket will even be passed on since it's not finished."

"I worry that someone years from now will find it and just toss it out," I said.

Then, simultaneously, we looked at each other with the same idea. Excitedly, we ran to the nursing station to enroll our other nurse colleagues into helping us with our plan. One nurse remembered a gold gift box left over from Christmas in our locker room. We lovingly wrapped up the unfinished blanket inside some tissue paper left over in the craft area of our unit. Together, we all wrote a letter to Meaghan from her mommy's nurses, telling her how hard her mommy had worked to finish the blanket and how sad she was that she could not finish it for her daughter. We suggested that maybe she could finish knitting the blanket herself. It could be a project that she and her mommy did together. We closed the letter by telling Meaghan how much we cared about her mommy and would always remember her for how much she loved her little girl. Then we wrapped the tissue around the blanket and the letter, placing them inside the box and closing the lid.

This simple act gave us, as nurses, a sense of peace. When we know children have lost one of their parents, it can be very difficult for us. Knowing we contributed to Meaghan's healing in this way helped us heal as well. Years later, I now see that we might have made a difference for Meaghan's mother, too, if we had we suggested helping her to write a letter and include it with the blanket, whether it was finished or not. Writing a letter to her daughter could have given her some peace at the end of her life, helping to relieve the frustration and fear she felt about not being able to finish this precious gift for her daughter in time.

QUESTIONS TO ASK YOURSELF

1. If you were this mother's nurse, how would you have supported her in completing the blanket?

2. What thoughts do you have about packing up a patient's personal belongings after their death?

3. What might be difficult for you to care for a young mother who is dying and how might you get some support for yourself, if you need it?

CHAPTER 7

REASSURING LOVED ONES WHO ARE NOT AT THE BEDSIDE

I could have waited to say goodbye
But couldn't bare to hear you cry
It was for you I chose my time
Sparing you the pain of watching me fly.

M. Dubetz

AFTER READING THIS CHAPTER

You will recognize opportunities to support family members who are not at their loved one's bedside when they die.

You will know how to appraise and maintain unit security after visiting hours.

OPPORTUNITIES FOR SHARING

As caregivers, we always have the opportunity to write a little note for the patient's family and leave it by their bedside. I remember one patient who kept a journal beside her bed so visitors could let the family know they had been there. Many of those who came in began to write loving words and memories about what the woman meant to them. When family members came in, they would eagerly read who had visited and what they had written. The woman herself was in poor health, so she couldn't talk with her visitors or family very long. The journal for visitors was a wonderful way to capture visits and memories.

During one nightshift, I found my patient wide-awake in the middle of the night looking at a beautiful bouquet of flowers on her bedside table. I bent over close and whispered that carnations were one of my favorite flowers, asking her who had brought them. Her roommate was sleeping, so I didn't want to wake her. However, I also did not want to leave my other patient lying wide awake without connecting with her.

"They're from my daughter," she whispered back. "It was her birthday today. She's always sent me flowers to thank me for being her mother."

She told me that, after many miscarriages, her daughter's birth had been a blessing.

"One child was enough," she said. "She's the most loving child I could ever have hoped for."

I pulled a chair up close to the head of her bed, so we could continue our quiet conversation. She then told me other thoughtful things that her daughter did to support her, and I agreed that they certainly did have a loving relationship. We spoke for a little longer, and I then made sure she was comfortable, encouraging her to sleep.

The woman's health deteriorated rapidly. The next night, she was no longer conscious. Before I went home, I picked up the journal she had at her bedside and decided to write in it. I told my patient's daughter about the conversations that her mother and I had shared. I wrote how much her mother loved her and saw their relationship as not lacking in anything. I continued to write about how grateful she was as a mother to have her daughter in her life. I let her daughter know that sending her mother flowers on her birthday inspired me to send flowers on my next birthday to thank my own mother. I ended my note by assuring her that her mother had been comfortable during the night, and although I had never met her daughter, I would remember the loving connection she and her mother had together.

This patient passed away on my days off. A couple of months later, when I was at work, I was paged to the front desk for a phone call. I did not recognize the caller's name on the other end, but she reminded me about her mother and that I had written in the journal. She asked if I could meet her at the coffee shop across the street after work for a short visit. I felt a warm friendly connection listening to her voice, so I agreed.

I did not have any trouble finding her because I had seen her photograph sitting on her mother's bedside table. She immediately stood up with a warm, inviting smile, opening her arms to greet me with a long hug. Her eyes filled with tears as she invited me to sit down. She must have been there for some time since she had almost finished drinking a cup of coffee. She asked me if she could get me a coffee and went to get two more.

"It's wonderful to meet someone I've heard so much about," I told her.

"I want you to know what a difference your note in my mother's journal made for me. It is helping me through my grief," she said. "When I can't sleep at night, I open the journal and read. I felt comforted and more connected to my mother when I read what you and what other's wrote."

My patient's daughter had three small children, and it was not possible for her to be with her mother during the night.

"It helps me feel less guilty knowing that someone like you was there with her when I couldn't be."

I told her again how much it meant to me that on her birthday, she had thought to give her mother flowers. I also said that I had shared this idea with a friend of mine, and we both wanted to send our mothers flowers on our own birthdays. Although she promised to connect again and let me know how she was doing, I knew she would not. She needed to move forward and heal on her own path.

Writing a short entry in my patient's journal was easy. At the time, I never realized it would help someone heal from grief. After that experience, I have taken the opportunity to leave a little note for other family members who were not able to spend the night with their loved ones. I knew that even though family members were home sleeping, they would likely not rest peacefully knowing their loved one was in the hospital and very unwell. A few words from the nurse who was caring for their family member during the night might make the following night easier for them.

QUESTIONS TO ASK YOURSELF

1. Practice writing a short note to a family member about your patient's night.

2. Would you feel comfortable meeting a family member after work? Why or why not?

3. Has a patient's family given you insight into your own life like the flowers my patient's daughter sent her mom?

HONORING THE DECISION TO LEAVE A LOVED ONE'S BEDSIDE

Leaving a loved one's bedside can also be a choice that family and loved ones make. Not everyone can sit and listen to the sounds of difficult breathing and watch their loved one waste away. Many find it difficult to adapt to the odor that impending death often brings. During this stage, family members may also feel powerless. Their loved one is dying, and they feel there is nothing they can do to support them.

As nurses, we try our best to offer explanations and comfort, but, regardless of our efforts, sometimes explanations just are not enough. Allowing family members to express their feelings and frustrations can help alleviate some of their emotional burden. Giving permission and reassurance to family members who feel they need to leave will greatly support them after their loved one has died. Otherwise, they may feel lingering guilt for not remaining at the person's bedside. I encourage loved ones to call me for a progress report. Allowing a family member or loved one to leave with a clear conscience is a gift you can give them.

I may say, "I know it's difficult for you to stay here beside your mother's bedside. I also know that it's difficult for you to make the choice to leave. Remember the choice you are making right now is because of the circumstances you are facing right now. Honor your decision and when you look back at this time, remember that your decision, although difficult, was one that you had to make."

Then I make sure the family member has a contact number for counseling support for any future support they may need.

In 2007, I read about volunteers staying with patients who are alone and dying. A nurse, Sandra Clarke, initiated this program in Oregon. After one of her patients asked her to sit with him, she reassured him that she would return after she assessed the rest of her patients. However, when she returned, the man had died. Her initiative started after this experience. Volunteers signed up for three to four-hour shifts to sit with patients who were alone. What an amazing gift to give those who have no one's hand to hold when leaving this world.

This may also support family members who cannot be at the bedside due to circumstances, or who choose not to be at the bedside offering direct comfort. Family members can feel greatly alleviated from their guilt, knowing that their loved one is not alone.

People experience and express their grief in many different ways—some of them startling. On one night shift, the elevator door opened, and a man in his thirties came to the desk. The nurses at the desk asked if we could help him.

"It's the first anniversary of my wife's death. She passed away here, and I wonder if I could just stand outside the door where she died—for just a moment."

It was a difficult decision for us to make, even though his request was simple. The unit was quiet. He seemed polite, well dressed, and genuine, so we gave him permission to have his moment. One of the nurses walked with him down the hall to the room where his wife had passed. The three other nurses on duty could see him from the desk as he stood for a moment in front of the closed door. The nurse who had escorted him stood a few feet away, allowing him some personal space.

Then, suddenly, the howl that came out of this man's mouth I can only describe as chilling. I have watched many family members react to their loved one's death. Nothing prepared me for the raw emotion this man exhibited, even a year after his wife's passing. He fell on the floor and continued sobbing. The nurse with him immediately kneeled down next to him while the rest of us rushed to help. Concerned about waking our other patients and disrupting the unit, we made soft hushing sounds as we put our arms under his shoulders and encouraged him to get up. Unfortunately, he was not ready to leave. We had to call security to escort him from the hospital.

I have no idea if this man's painful grief subsided, or if he tried to contact our unit again. I can only hope that, with time and support, he found acceptance and peace.

QUESTIONS TO ASK YOURSELF

1. What would you say to a family who had been vigilant at the bedside but were not there when their loved one died?

2. What type of support, if any, is available on your unit for patients who are alone?

3. What could you say to family members who cannot be at their loved one's bedside due to work or other circumstances?

CHAPTER 8

DON'T JUDGE YOUR PATIENTS BY THE MASK THEY WEAR

To be beautiful means to be yourself.
You don't need to be accepted by others.
You need to accept yourself.

—*Thich Nhat Hanh*

AFTER READING THIS CHAPTER

You will connect with your patient's needs, regardless of their life choices.

You will demonstrate empathy while delivering care to your patient.

IT'S WHAT'S INSIDE THAT COUNTS

Mitzy walked into our unit for admission and all our jaws dropped—at least I know mine did. She was only 5'3" tall, but you would have thought she was 6' the way she strolled up to our desk. She had perfected a sensual walk, probably over years of practice.

Mitzy was a prostitute.

We didn't know where to look first. The short skirt that barely covered her buttocks, her low-cut blouse, revealing a lacy push-up bra, or her black stiletto shoes. When I saw those spiked heels, I silently wondered whether she had back problems. Her eyes were fringed with extra-long false lashes, and her bleached blonde hair reached down to her waist with the help of professionally twisted extensions. She wore a pale foundation that contrasted with her bright red pouty lips.

"Please call me Mitzy," she said in a sultry voice, after giving her last name. Mitzy was my admission, so I escorted her down to her private room where she would be spending the next few months. I felt my peers stare at us as we walked down the hall, Mitzy pulling her zebra-striped suitcase while the sound of her heels clipped audibly over the small wheels of the blood pressure machine I was pushing. After unpacking, Mitzy put on a hospital gown, our signature attire, according to hospital protocol. She replaced her towering black footwear with her own fluffy pink slippers and matching pink housecoat. Even though she placed her spiked heels in a bedside cupboard, she still maintained her own style.

I usually look at a patient with the thought, "This could be my daughter or my mother," which helps me feel more connected to the person. However, no matter how hard I tried, I could not think of one family member or friend I could say connected to her. Mitzy's lifestyle was beyond anything I had ever seen—except on television.

I reviewed the procedure of her bone marrow transplant, had her sign the consent form, and took her blood pressure, temperature, weight, height, and oxygen saturation count. Then I asked her if she had any questions for me. She turned her face to me and for a moment, I got a glimpse of what was underneath her façade when she asked, "I will be okay after all of this, right?"

"You know," I assured her, "we have really good results with this kind of treatment." I actually did not know how she was going to fare, but I didn't want to add to her fear. I responded with the safest answer to reassure her and to keep her positive.

People ask me this question many times and in many different situations. What lies underneath all our emotions and questions is our biggest fear—the fear of dying. Even with the assurance that death is the means to a reward in eternity, human beings may still experience some fear, either of leaving others behind, of unfinished business, or of a painful death.

Mitzy's question was no different. I have found the best way to answer these questions is to tell patients what I know. I did know that this treatment had good results and that many did very well with the treatments. I trusted Mitzy's outcome would be positive. However, I have no crystal ball to tell the future, and my patients know that. What they are looking for is a lifeline to give them some comfort.

Although I could not connect with Mitzy by imagining her as one of my family members, I could empathize with the question she asked, knowing I, or anyone else, would want the answer. Her question caused a shift in me and my perception of Mitzy. She ended up having a difficult time with the chemotherapy regime before her bone marrow transplant infusion. Over the weeks, we witnessed a dramatic physical change in her. The peroxided hair, complete with extensions, fell out almost overnight. After her first episode of vomiting, Mitzy had no energy for putting on make-up. Even applying lipstick was too much of a chore. The steroids infused into her veins filled her face with a puffiness that took away any resemblance to what she looked like when she first entered the hospital. She developed mouth and lip sores, making it too painful to speak. Mitzy communicated mostly by writing, but attempting to ask for what she wanted in writing took too long, or she wouldn't have the energy to write it, which frustrated her.

Mitzy's body reacted to her bone marrow (graft versus host disease). Her once porcelain-looking skin developed dark dry patches and some open sores. Her feet were swollen, and the edema traveled halfway up her leg. Her cozy fuzzy slippers had not fit her for some time, so nursing staff replaced them with a pair of paper slip-ons. Her matching pink housecoat was in a bag, needing to be washed after one of her episodes of vomiting. Now she wore a one-size-fits-all unisex cover-up. There was no more evidence of the Mitzy who had first walked onto our unit. The treatments had stripped away all her style. Chemotherapy and the bone marrow transplant had not been kind to her.

Over the next several weeks, Mitzy's mouth sores started to improve, the swelling in her feet had started to go down, and a small amount of reddish curly hair began to appear. Regardless of the positive physical changes, she showed no signs of a positive response to her treatment. The hematologist came into her room early one morning. He glanced at the board on her wall with its history of blood counts. Then he turned to talk with Mitzy. She looked like a little girl sitting on her bed, once again in her pink slippers and fuzzy robe. He told her, in a soft sympathetic voice, that her response to her treatments had failed and that he was sorry, but there were no other options for her. She nodded slowly and then asked, "How long do I have?"

"It's difficult to say. Perhaps a few weeks. I'm very sorry," he said.

When he asked her if she had any more questions, Mitzy shook her head and looked away.

No visitors had ever come up before that day. Occasionally she received phone calls from friends asking about her status. Mitzy appeared to be alone on her journey. But on this day, a rather short, maternal-looking woman in her mid-fifties came to the desk and asked for Mitzy's room. We wondered who this could be and watched as she followed the directions the unit clerk gave her to Mitzy's room.

The woman turned out to be Mitzy's mother. After she arrived, whatever had taken place in the past was reconciled. Mitzy's mom began spending most of her day and every night with her daughter. Mitzy appeared grateful for her mother's presence and support. Often we would come into the room to find them holding hands or her mother rubbing Mitzy's back. She referred to her daughter as "Karen," so one of the nurses asked Mitzy if she would like the staff to call her Karen as well.

"Yes," she said. "I would prefer that."

Karen had returned, so we knew Mitzy was gone and would never come back.

The chemotherapy and transplant had stripped away Karen's blood counts along with the masquerade that Mitzy had been playing out for so long. Even though her treatments failed, Karen cherished the love and comfort of her mother's return to her life and the sense of peace and power she achieved at her life's end.

QUESTIONS TO ASK YOURSELF

1. How would you relate to caring for someone with an alternative life style?

2. What words of comfort would you use to support a patient who is physically changing due to treatment?

3. When a patient asks you how they might respond to treatment, what could you say?

CHAPTER 9

YOU CAN HELP MAKE DREAMS COME TRUE

While they all fall in love with her smile,
She waits for one who will fall in love with her scars.

—*The Dreamer*

AFTER READING THIS CHAPTER

You will relate to your patients and what is important to them at the end of their life.

You will recognize opportunities to enroll others in achieving a goal.

A HOSPITAL WEDDING

Katie was a 40-year-old mother of three children under the age of five and in a loving relationship with the children's father, but they had never married.

"We never seemed to find the money or the time to get married," she told Celestee, her primary nurse in our department. "We were always busy with something, and it wasn't a priority."

The day before, Katie's partner had brought her to the emergency department because she was increasingly becoming short of breath with a history of a chronic cough and tightness in her chest that had been bothersome for about three months. An ultrasound showed a pulmonary embolus, and further test results showed lung cancer had spread to her liver, bones, and her brain. The blood clot could be treated, but sadly, the cancer had spread where only palliative radiation could be offered for symptom control.

Katie, and her partner John met Celestee in the radiation department of our center. Celestee asked Katie standard questions about her current pain medication, the effectiveness of the medications, and side effects. At first, John refused the offer of palliative home care, saying he had things handled at home. When Celestee explained the role of home care and the 24/7 service they offer, John agreed, realizing he could then return to work. They had disability insurance, which helped, but it was not as much as they needed.

Our main focus, as nurses, is assessing and taking care of our patient's physical needs. A patient in pain is not often able to answer our questions because the focus will be on the pain and the family member's attention will be on their loved one. As nurses, we must address a patient's comfort level first in order to assess their health issues properly. When Celestee met with Katie and John, Katie rated her pain about a two out of ten. Before going to the emergency department, Katie had rated her pain as eight out of ten. Celestee now knew that Katie was receiving good pain control and could continue her questions.

At the end of the assessment interview, Celestee asked Katie, "If there was anything that would make a difference in your life, either physically or psychologically, what would that be?"

This question empowers the patients to say what matters most to them. I once asked a patient this question, and she told me she wanted to die in her homeland of India. She realized that before she passed on, her greatest wish was to see her family members again. This patient was palliative and had only a few weeks left to live. Medical staff had to make copies of her treatment summary, provide adequate pain medication, and provide her with a letter from our physician supporting her use of these narcotics. The family purchased the airline ticket for her. Then it was our turn to call the airline and arrange for her oxygen. Sometimes making a patient's wish possible is a race against time. I've been known to enroll the support of other medical staff to help me fulfill patients' wishes.

When Celestee asked Katie what she would most like, Katie said, "I would like to get married." Then she looked at her lifelong partner and her children's father. He nodded yes. With that one question, Celestee gave Katie permission to say what she had wanted for several years. Katie's eyes lit up with excitement as she gave Celestee permission to plan a wedding in our hospital for the next day.

Celestee asked her coworkers for help, and everyone immediately went into action. The hospital chaplain agreed to perform the service in the hospital chapel. It happened to be administration week, so secretaries all over the unit happily donated bouquets of flowers on their desks to Katie for her wedding.

The day arrived, and the bride and her future husband joyously checked in at the reception desk. Staff members on our unit were alive with excitement, too. Katie and John didn't want to make a fuss, so they decided to get married in their everyday clothes. Celestee had waved her magic wand. The chapel was ready, and the chaplain performed the ceremony. Everyone cried.

Celestee made a connection with her patient that went beyond the usual professional questions we ask. Many nurses, short on staff and with an increasing number of patients, only find time to do necessary tasks. We rarely experience moments with our patients to have a deeper connection. Hospital leaders recognized Celestee with an award for the difference she made. She humbly accepted, reminding all of us what nursing excellence looks like and what our jobs are really about.

QUESTIONS TO ASK YOURSELF

1. What could you say to a patient to ensure that the time they have left empowers and pleases them or gives them peace?

2. When a patient expresses a wish, would you be able to do anything to help make that happen?

3. What could you say or do that could help to ensure your patient is coping as well as possible with their situation?

CHAPTER 10

WHEN YOU GET PERSONALLY INVOLVED WITH YOUR PATIENTS

Remember
I will still be here
As long as you hold me
In your memory

—*Josh Groban*

AFTER READING THIS CHAPTER

You will learn what it means to "dance on your patient's dance floor."

You will demonstrate professional relationships with your patients and be aware of the impact of becoming personally involved with their end-of-life journey.

THE MUSTANG GIRLS

I heard Taunya before I saw her. Her laughter echoed down the hall of our radiation department. I wondered who was in such a good mood. As I got closer to the reception desk, I saw the person responsible for all the merriment.

Taunya stood wearing a shocking fuchsia pink wig, a big pair of oversized fake glasses, her head tossed back in laughter. My new patient turned to meet me.

"Hi! I'm Taunya," she said loudly.

Taunya had been diagnosed with a Stage 4 brain tumor a few weeks before I met her. She had completed her surgery and was now on the next path of her treatment: six weeks, five days a week, for 30 radiation treatments to her brain. I wondered if her hyperactive mannerism was the result of a personality change after her surgery, or perhaps a side effect of steroids, which can also alter a person's behavior. I soon found out that Taunya always lived life with high energy. Her husband quietly stood to her side, sheepishly smiling and dressed like the Mad Hatter from *Alice in Wonderland*, enjoying her fun.

I introduced myself to Taunya and her husband Phil. Then I asked them if they would come with me so that I could get a history and do some teaching with them. Taunya said she needed to go to the washroom first, so Phil and I waited out in the hallway for her. A few minutes later, Taunya came out of the washroom. She took my hand as if we had been friends for years. Her hands were wet.

"I'm glad you washed your hands," I said, jokingly.

"I didn't!" she replied. Then she burst into laughter.

That was the beginning of me watching Taunya live her life powerfully. Phil said his wife celebrated every holiday to the fullest extent possible. At Halloween, they went all out decorating their home inside and out, with Phil's collection of vintage cars sitting in the back yard. Behind the wheels of these automobiles, "wrapped mummies" appeared ready to take the vehicle for a spin around town. They both giggled when they shared how Phil would sometimes wrap himself completely up in gauze, climb into one of the cars, and as the neighborhood children approached, he would turn his head to greet them. Christmas was no different. People drove miles to admire the decorations and light show that surrounded their home. Obviously, regardless of Taunya's devastating circumstances, she could still have fun and play in her life.

I listened as they told me how their lives had changed drastically after the fatal news the doctors gave them. The diagnosis and Taunya's short life expectancy of a maximum of one-and-a-half years to live left them in shock.

Up until then, they lived a comfortable life in a completely renovated heritage home in a small town. They had moved from Ontario, leaving family and friends behind. They enjoyed their life. Phil worked as a heavy-duty mechanic, spending his time off work fixing up the antique cars he collected. Taunya worked at an office job and loved to cook. She felt passionate about her relationships with the few new friends she had made. They were happy.

After the diagnosis and the overwhelming news that Taunya would most likely not see her 35th birthday, they came up with a plan. Phil would quit his well-paying job. They would sell their home and then move to a remote area. A smaller house farther away from the city would have them debt free with no pressure on Phil to work. They wanted to spend the little time they had left together.

I was shocked when they told me how cold and opportunistic the realtor they hired had been when they sold their home. She had encouraged them to accept her offer to buy their house under the pretense of helping them out, so they could move quickly. A few weeks later, that same realtor flipped the house for a large profit. It was unbelievable to me that someone could take advantage of another human being under these circumstances. Phil and Taunya did not want to spend the little bit of time or energy they had to engage in a lawsuit. I felt humbled when Phil told me that both he and Taunya trusted in karma. More important things were at stake other than revenge.

I felt a connection with Taunya and Phil soon after meeting them. When I was in nursing school, our instructors told us we should avoid "dancing on our patients' dance floors." In other words, we were to remain professional and not get personally involved with our patients.

According to our nursing instructors, every individual and every family has their own particular dance they perform. We all learn our "dances" at a young age under the influence of parents, teachers, pastors, and others. As medical personnel, we have our own dances, they said. Our nursing instructors sent this message to us loud and clear: Never dance on your patient's dance floor and never allow them to dance on yours. Maintain a professional relationship. You can feel empathy—that is compassion, understanding, and putting yourself in your patient's place—but do not get emotionally involved with your patients.

I would break this golden rule with Taunya.

I'm not sure why, but I made a conscious decision to show Taunya and Phil what I was really like after taking off my nursing cap. With them, I felt a sense of freedom. Our discussions moved from cautious and deliberately professional to casual. All three of us could say what we thought and felt. No longer did I feel I had to have all the answers. I could let them see that I too felt angry about the way our health care system was organized. In a more patient-orientated medical system, people would not have to wait long hours in order to receive a simple prescription.

I shifted from being an advocate to change our broken health care system to being this couple's personal support. I was on their side, and I got to know them personally. For example, Taunya's 1969 Mustang was her pride and joy. She told me that the most frustrating part of her life right now was not being allowed to drive her car. Her illness had started with seizures, and the surgeon had said that she would not be able to operate a vehicle again until she was seizure-free for one year. That was the law. If she broke it, her insurance would not cover her if she were in an accident.

It did not take a mathematician to figure out that given Taunya's life expectancy, she would not be driving again.

"Losing my hair, my energy, my home is nothing compared to losing my freedom to drive my car," she shared. "I love my car."

Taunya's vehicle sat in her backyard, taunting her with the reminder of the freedom she felt driving it. Sitting on her porch in her lounge chair, she fixated on her beloved Mustang. Then she got up, opened the car door, and sat in the driver's seat. The car key was on the visor and magically dropped onto her lap. Without hesitation, she inserted it into the ignition and turned the starter. Reclining her head back, eyes closed, she inhaled the recognizable smell of the leather seats, listened to the soft purring of the motor, and allowed the familiar vibrations of the car to surround her.

Phil was watching from the side of the yard. Throwing caution to the wind, he jumped into the passenger seat and encouraged Taunya to put the stick shift into first gear. She didn't need to be told twice. The intimate, joyful, familiar experience had them both giggling like schoolchildren skipping class. Taunya accelerated the engine and expertly steered her car on to the country road in front of their house. They told me that they were both grinning from ear to ear as they drove away from their reality.

As I put myself in Taunya's place, I realized being restricted from driving would be devastating. The frustration of seeing her vehicle so near and yet so far made Taunya realize her limiting circumstances even more. Listening to her talk about her experience, I got a glimpse of what Taunya's life was like. Taunya shared with me how she could leave all the fears and experiences of the last month behind by simply taking a short drive down a deserted country road. Taking the wheel of her car was like taking control of her life—even for just a moment. I watched her eyes light up telling me about feeling free. Although I would never encourage a patient to disobey a doctor's order, I was secretly pleased she and Phil had broken a rule and went for their joyrides.

When I was single, I owned a 1966 Mustang. I always felt regret for having traded in a red classic Mustang for a white Toyota station wagon. At the time, it seemed more responsible for me to drive a reliable family car rather than an impractical sports car. I was a new mother and felt I needed to look the part. Placing my baby into a red Mustang didn't seem like a good choice for a mother with an infant. So, I let my dream car go. I shared my story with Phil and Taunya.

"I hope I get the opportunity to buy another Mustang one day," I said.

The next words Taunya said shook me to my core.

"What are you waiting for?" she asked.

I thought about what she said for the rest of the day and went home after work. I told my husband I was not waiting any longer. I would be fulfilling my dream of buying another classic Mustang.

The next day, my husband and I drove to a nearby town to look at a 1966 Mustang for sale. The minute I saw it, I reached for my checkbook and bought it. I didn't even negotiate. I could not wait to share my news with Taunya and Phil on Monday.

When I told them about my new purchase, we were no longer patient, husband, and nurse, but new friends who shared a mutual passion beyond the confining walls of the cancer center. We had a deeper level of connection. Taunya and Phil thought it would be a great idea for me to show them my new car and invited me out to their place for the next weekend. I said yes and with that, officially "stepped onto their dance floor." My professional role had changed. I was still Taunya's nurse, but I was now allowing them to get a glimpse of who I was at the end of the day when my lab coat came off. I had no problem moving onto their dance floor, but now I was allowing them to step onto mine as well.

My dance floor was complete as we enjoyed wine, laughing at jokes (especially after the wine). I was not that starched professional nurse I had to play at work. My nursing cap felt more comfortable tilting a little off center. The more I revealed about who I really was, the more all three of us relaxed. Regardless of any doubt I experienced about crossing a professional boundary, my decision led to an amazing friendship and an incredible connection with no regrets. Making a conscious choice to shift from a professional to a more personal relationship and sharing myself more personally to Taunya and Phil gave me a sense of freedom. Our discussions moved from cautious and well thought out to conversations during which we could all say what we felt. I no longer had the sense they expected me to have all the answers.

Over the next several months, Taunya's condition deteriorated, and Phil flew to Turkey twice to purchase a medication that had shown promising results for prolonging the life of people with brain tumors. He had to arrange for someone to stay with Taunya since he would be gone for a few days. A friend agreed to support them and move into the house during his absence. When Phil returned with the medication, he told me he had to inject it intramuscularly, but he had no idea how to do this. No doctor or nurse would legally administer a foreign medication for him. Using an orange for a mock hip, a nurse they knew showed Phil how to inject, draw back for blood, and push the medication in.

Despite the faith they both had, these daily injections made no difference. Taunya's health continued to deteriorate.

Supportive care in the community was minimal and frustrating. Having a stranger come into their home and provide nursing care for Taunya frustrated Phil. The schedules never coincided with the routine he had set up with Taunya. Supplies, even a turning sheet, were not available to assist her in changing position.

One evening, Phil had to bring Taunya into the emergency department. The medication she was taking failed to relieve her headaches. Phil had no choice but to drive Taunya into town and have her assessed. A steroid medication Taunya was taking caused her to gain weight, especially in her abdomen. The nurse at the triage desk who called them forward immediately assumed Taunya was in labor. Taunya's embarrassment and Phil's frustration escalated. Why did they have to go through this upsetting hospital visit?

After returning to the sanctuary of their home, a week later Taunya became blind in one eye. Phil moved the furniture in their bedroom so she could watch TV and look at special treasures or photographs on her dresser with her good eye. She became increasingly weak and spent most of her time in bed. Phil moved her Mustang to the side of the house so she could see it out the window from her bed. Moving her to the toilet became too difficult for both of them, so Taunya remained in bed with Phil changing incontinent pads. Their already close relationship grew to a deeper level.

As the brain tumor grew, Taunya went completely blind. Her headaches became more severe, so doctors increased her steroids, which kept her more awake than asleep and kept Phil from resting because he made himself available 24 hours a day for all his wife's needs. Occasionally he would go outside and start Taunya's Mustang, so she could enjoy the sound of the motor running, which would always make her smile. Few visitors came to see them. Neither Phil nor Taunya's families had the financial means to come for a visit. Phil cared for Taunya on his own.

Ultimately, Phil broke his promise to Taunya to keep her at home until the end. He could no longer manage controlling the pain of her headaches or care for her on his own. The home care where they lived was not equipped to handle a hospice patient full time, so Phil had no choice but to have Taunya admitted to their small-town palliative care unit.

Phil was devastated when he watched his wife transferred by ambulance out of their home. He felt he had failed to fulfill his pledge that Taunya would die in their bed with the wedding photo of the two of them hanging above their headboard. He felt he had reneged on their plan that Taunya would have the familiar smells of her house, the soft purring of her beloved Mustang's motor, and the loving touch of her husband to comfort her at the end. Phil had no other options. A few days later, Taunya passed away, surrounded by suction tubes, the sound of call bells, IV pumps, and the unfamiliar voices of nursing staff and physicians.

Her funeral took place during a snowstorm, preventing most of their few friends and me to attend. It seemed fitting that this couple, who lived their lives mostly alone, would share this last day together with few others around them.

In many rural communities, hospice resources are often limited. If complications arise at the end of patients' lives, those who want to stay home to die have no choice but to move into a hospital. Unfortunately, hospital costs far exceed the cost of a palliative care home visit. An established outreach program from a hospital to this community would have been a great asset in this case to meet the important needs of patients such as Taunya.

Eventually, life moves on, and Phil's life was no different.

After Taunya's death, he could not see a future worth living for himself. Everything that mattered to him had revolved around his wife and their relationship. Now he was alone. How can someone pick up the pieces of his life when he loses someone he loves and is an extension of himself? With no standard steps for anyone to take, Phil, like thousands of other grieving spouses, put one foot in front of the other on an unfamiliar road. He slowly moved forward alone into an unknown future.

Phil began the challenging process of starting a new life. First, he sold all their personal possessions. No longer wanting the reminder of materialistic memories, Phil got rid of everything that he and Taunya had together. If items did not sell, he gave them away or burned them in their backyard fire pit. Phil was angry when another opportunistic buyer gave him a ridiculously low-ball offer on the house. His response this time made his feelings heard loud and clear. Phil threatened to burn the house down or give it away before he would ever deal with this individual.

Phil then began a two-year trip through Europe, Australia, and Asia. He filled up his backpack with necessities and left only a small box of photos behind. I was one of the few people who heard from him regularly. His short messages just included basic information about which country he was in and his next travel plan. Over time, his emails became more intimate, including powerful photos of his experiences. I sensed that Phil was on a healing pilgrimage, not an escape journey.

Two years after Taunya's death, Phil returned home to introduce my husband and me to Natasha. Phil had met her on the last few months of his backpacking trip. They connected as backpacking and traveling companions, but their friendship grew into committed love.

Their meeting was no accident. Natasha had been on her own healing journey after the death of her close friend—Taunya.

QUESTIONS TO ASK YOURSELF

1. How do you maintain appropriate boundaries between you and your patients?

2. What would you say to a patient who asks you to come to her house for dinner to thank you for your care?

3. You will relate to some of your patients better than others. What draws you to a closer relationship?

CHAPTER 11

YOU CAN LEARN TO LIVE FROM YOUR PATIENTS FACING DEATH

Everything that has a beginning has an ending.
Make your peace with that—
And all will be well.

— *Buddha*

AFTER READING THIS CHAPTER

You will identify your own learning opportunities through your patient's end of life experience.

You will review your own belief about living your own life powerfully.

CHOOSING LAUGHTER OVER TEARS

Kim was 17 years old when she came into my life. She arrived, accompanied by her mother, to our center for radiation treatments for her Stage 4 brain tumor. She had experienced a seizure a month before and an MRI revealed a large growth on her brain. Doctors immediately performed surgery and sent a sample of the tumor to the pathology department. The results were grim. Despite current treatment options, Kim had less than a year to live.

During her radiation treatments, I was assigned to care for her, ensuring she was managing well and assessing any side effects she might experience. Kim's radiation oncologist had her remain on steroids, even after her surgery, because the radiation treatments could cause her brain to swell. The steroids would minimize any side effects such as headaches. However, the steroids had their own list of adverse effects. Kim constantly felt hungry, ate more, and gained weight. She also experienced insomnia, another side effect of the steroids. With the extra weight and sleeplessness, Kim was finding it difficult to be active, which meant she gained more weight and was caught in a vicious circle.

I wondered how Kim was coping. I know self-image is very important to teenage girls. Kim had already lost some hair near the surgical site, and now she would lose the rest of her hair with the radiation.

"It will grow back," she said after I asked her what her thoughts were around her hair loss.

I was impressed with Kim's courageous, matter-of-fact response.

While coming in to our center for daily treatments, Kim had a difficult time staying in school. Her teachers arranged for her to do most of her homework at home. Kim's mother would drive to the school, hand in the assignments, and pick up new ones. The family lived on a farm about 20 minutes from the nearest town. Kim's connection with her friends became less during treatments and she spent many of her days and evenings at home with her mother. Kim's father worked as a long-distance truck driver; her two sisters were both away at college.

I was easily drawn to Kim's personality and her cute lopsided smile. She always had a quick wit and sarcastic sense of humor. However, her stamina left those of us caring for her amazed. Rarely did we see this kind of staying power in adult patients, let alone in a person this young. Her daily two-hour drive to our center did nothing to lower her energy or diminish her good mood.

Kim's tumor encompassed a large area of her brain, making it necessary to radiate an extensive area of her skull, which included the areas near her eyes. Within two weeks of radiation, Kim lost her sight, but she took being blind in stride, too, never losing her ability to joke and laugh. When checking in before her daily treatments, she would tell the receptionist that she had driven the car into town that day. This was always followed by her lovely little giggle and those within hearing would laugh along with her. She never got tired of that joke, and we never got tired of hearing it. Kim had a joyful energy and a gift to lift the spirits of everyone around her, regardless of the circumstances.

Even though Kim knew she had a brain tumor and was undergoing radiation to treat any residual tumor left after her surgery, she never asked whether her prognosis was terminal. She showed up every day as if life was an adventure with a chance to chat and visit with all of us.

As she gained weight, lost her sight and her hair, Kim was never aware that people sometimes looked at her with pity. She usually arrived in a wheelchair pushed by her mother Karen, since Kim found it more difficult every day to walk from the parking lot. The steroids also made Kim feel extremely warm. She would often wear sleeveless shirts. Her skin began showing deep, wide purple lines of strain from the tissue stretching. Her feet also began to swell—another side effect, which she dealt with by wearing comfortable fuzzy slippers instead of shoes.

Karen once told me she was secretly glad Kim could no longer see. She did not want her daughter to notice the looks that strangers gave her. Above all, she did not want Kim to be able to see herself in the mirror because she no longer resembled the way she looked before her illness

Kim cared about her schoolwork and kept up with her studies. With the help of her family, Kim managed to complete her assignments. She also had an unwavering belief in God. The family's minister visited regularly at Kim's home to support her spiritual practice. The Canadian

National Institute for the Blind gave her a computer with a Braille keyboard, allowing her the ability to keep in touch with family and friends through e-mail. She even learned to crochet and did a better job than many who can see. I have a table runner she made for me, and there is not one mistake on it.

Instead of reading and watching television, Kim now filled the hours of her days by working at her computer, crocheting, and listening to television. In addition, Kim loved to help her mother with the daily chores. She fed the baby lambs and goats and made sure the dogs and cats received their necessary attention. Kim mastered the art of baking as well, and always made sure her family and visitors had homemade cookies. If friends could not come physically, they would call Kim on the phone. Kim never complained about the daily radiation treatments she underwent, and no one had to remind her to take her oral chemotherapy pills. When people asked her how she was doing, she always told them she was doing fine. She was never negative about her circumstances.

"I'm blind and I have a tumor," she would say, "and there's nothing I can do about it." Then she would smile her lopsided little grin.

Kim depended on her mother, and Karen was always by her side. Even when Kim went to the washroom or had a shower, her mom was no more than an arm's length away. They also took afternoon naps together and shared the same bed, in case Kim needed anything during the night.

About two months after completing her radiation treatments, the "Make a Wish Foundation" granted Kim's wish to plan a Caribbean cruise together with her family. Kim needed a nurse to accompany her on this trip. She asked me if I would come. I felt honored she had chosen me. This became the second time I crossed that invisible line that I was warned about in nursing school: "Do not get on your patients' dance floors." I always thought this rule about keeping your distance from your patients must have come from the early twentieth-century rather than modern-day thinking.

I wondered, "How could I possibly make a connection with anyone without knowing their particular dance?"

I broke the unwritten rule and spent ten days sitting at the pool, going on day excursions, and having every meal with Kim and her family. My relationship with them grew very close. This time with them on their family vacation allowed me to be better acquainted with Kim and her sisters, allowing them some individual time with me to tell me the impact that Kim's illness had on their lives. I was their sister's nurse who also became someone they could trust. After the cruise, I continued my close friendship with Kim and her family. We visited each other often. If they came into the city, they would schedule their plans so that we could meet for lunch. Occasionally, I drove out to their farm to visit them.

About six months after her treatments, I shared with Kim and Karen about a course that had the ability to empower and transform lives. I encouraged Kim to consider taking this weekend personal development course herself, hoping she would gain some independence. From my perspective, Kim's mother Karen had become as dependent on Kim as Kim had become on her, so I urged them to take the weekend course together. They accepted my invitation, and both had transformative experiences. By Sunday evening, Kim was unrecognizable from the person who had started the course on Friday morning. She no longer held on to her mother's hand or needed her mother within arm's reach. During the course, both mother and daughter found a way to stay connected without always being in each other's personal space.

Within two weeks, Kim found a house with an affordable upstairs area for rent and decided to move out of her family's home and into her own place more than an hour away from her mother. Kim was excited. The first thing she wanted was to get a cat to keep her company. She also joined a blind bowling league and made plans to go to school at a community college. The family hired a caregiver to check in with Kim every day, giving Kim's parents, some needed reassurance about their daughter's new independence and freedom.

Every six months Kim had an MRI. Her oncologists were in awe about how well she was doing. Time moved on, and her health stayed steadily positive with no change. Seven years after Kim had finished her treatments, she and I made plans for her to fly to Phoenix to stay with my husband and me for a week in our second home. She had never flown anywhere on her own and was determined to make this trip solo. We had made all our plans, Kim had purchased her plane tickets, obtained her medical documentation, and renewed her passport. However, several days before she was to make her first flight from Canada to the United States, Kim suffered three major seizures, one after another. The small hospital where she lived could not manage her symptoms. Flown immediately, to the nearest city's emergency department, an MRI revealed three new masses in her brain. Everyone was devastated. She was admitted onto a neurology unit, and the family discussed a plan for surgery with a team of doctors and specialists. It was mid-December, and the surgeon said he could wait until after Christmas to remove these tumors. In the meantime, Kim's seizures could be controlled with steroids and anti-seizure medication. He emphasized there would be no trip to Phoenix. It could be too dangerous.

Karen called me and told me the news about Kim's seizures and hospitalization. I knew Kim's prognosis was grim, having witnessed the mostly negative outcomes when patients have neuro surgery for the second or third time. However, nothing prepared me for Kim's heartbreaking phone call to me the next day. When I answered the phone, all I heard was her crying. She had been discharged home that morning

"It's not fair, Meina. It's just not fair!" she sobbed.

In all the time I had known Kim, I had never witnessed any signs of frustration or sadness. I had never heard her openly weep. Listening to her, I realized that Kim was not crying about the tumor having come back. She was upset because the surgeon had told her she could not come to Phoenix.

"That stupid doctor said I couldn't come," she stammered.

Even though I could hear how mad and frustrated Kim was, the nurse in me wanted to side with her surgeon and explain why she needed to follow his orders. However, I knew Kim personally. I also recognized what Kim was willing to risk her life for this opportunity, regardless of the consequences. I wanted to support her in whatever way I could. Traveling after she had surgery would be impossible. I understood that if Kim did not go now, she would never have the opportunity to make this trip.

To help Kim and her family weigh the consequences of embarking on this trip, I had a serious conversation with her mother about the possibility that her daughter could deteriorate and not make it back home, ending up in a hospital in the United States far away from her family. I could support Kim if she were here, but what about her mother and the rest of her family? What needs might Kim have if an emergency were to happen? Kim said she was willing to take the chance of coming down.

Karen said, "Kim's decision is all that matters. I agree with what she wants."

I told them both I would see what I could do. Then I would call them back. We had three days before the planned trip to organize everything and find a physician who would support us to make this happen. That evening I called Kim's radiation oncologist at home and told him what was happening with Kim. Dr. Husain immediately agreed that Kim should be on that flight and experience Phoenix. He said he would support her in any way he could and arranged a supply of additional medications in case Kim's symptoms got worse. Kim, her family, and I decided to create a game around this uncertainty. She loved the idea of playing the game we launched: "Kim goes to Phoenix." We all wanted to help make Kim's trip a reality.

Kim's mom and I had a more in-depth conversation about the strong possibility that Kim might become gravely ill during her trip and die in Arizona.

"I want this for Kim," her mother said. "Our family wants this for Kim. We're willing to take the risk."

Three days later, Kim was in the air and on her three-hour flight to Phoenix.

I waited anxiously in the terminal, staring down the long corridor where I knew Kim would be coming to from her gate. Eventually, I saw her and watched as the flight attendant pushed Kim in a wheelchair toward the public waiting area. This was one of Kim's bravest moments. Tears filled my eyes watching this courageous young woman follow her heart's desire and tapping into her inner strength to get here. As Kim got closer, I could hear her giggle as she shared something with the flight attendant. I was laughing as well when she got to me.

When she heard my voice, Kim said, "Hey, Meina! Guess what? They confiscated my crochet hook going through customs. I guess they thought a blind girl was going to hijack the plane."

Kim was very excited and happy, practically bouncing out of the wheelchair. We immediately called her mother and told her that her precious cargo had landed. All was well.

We spent the week buying souvenirs for her family, decorating the Christmas tree, going to Christmas parties in our neighborhood, and spending time on the sofa with our cat on her lap. She met many of our friends at a neighborhood Christmas brunch, and Kim spoke openly about her brain tumor and being blind.

I noticed she ended every conversation she had with anyone by saying, "I didn't listen to my doctor. I went to Phoenix even when he told me I couldn't go."

Our friends and neighbors were in awe of Kim's powerful attitude in spite of the many obstacles she faced. During her stay with us, my husband and I took many photographs of Kim in our back yard. We wanted to capture the fun time she was having in Phoenix. We didn't focus at all on the fact that these would most likely be our last pictures of her. In my favorite photo of Kim, we captured her sitting next to our water fountain, her face turned up to the sky, feeling the warmth of the sun on her skin. Of course, her little crooked grin peeked out of the picture as well.

The day before she left to go home, Kim and I talked frankly about the end of her life. She said she had no fear, no regrets, and she was at peace dying whenever that would happen. She believed that a better world was waiting for her, and, in that world, she would regain her sight and reunite with relatives and friends who had died.

I was glad that Kim could not see me crying.

Then she asked me if I knew she only had a year to live when I met her.

"Yes," I said. "I did."

"I just heard about that recently," she said. "It's a damn good thing they never told me before!" Then she laughed.

I think it was a good thing that she didn't know before as well. I believe that, by not knowing her fate, Kim lived moment by moment and never worried about what lay ahead. Our time together with Kim was over too soon. She packed her suitcase with gifts and souvenirs for her family members back home, excited to return to Canada and share her week with her family.

It was time to say goodbye. Kim was never one to express her affection with a kiss. She had rarely ever even given anyone a hug, and then only if the person getting the hug had actually asked for one. When we hugged, Kim turned her head and kissed me on my cheek.

"And that's the only one you will get from me," she joked.

I laughed and watched the attendant wheel her to her gate.

Kim enjoyed Christmas 2009 with her family and immediately afterwards had surgery to remove her tumors. Unfortunately, during surgery, the surgeon discovered a fourth tumor in a location where it would be unsafe to remove. He could do nothing else for her. Kim was discharged a week later to her home, where her mother could care for her. In March, when she required more support, the family moved her to a palliative care ward in her hometown.

When I returned to Calgary from Phoenix, I saw Kim a few days before she died at the end of April 2010. My husband and I pulled up to the little hospital in the small town near their farm where she had been admitted. I could feel my tears well up before I even got to her unit, but I managed to pull myself together before entering her room.

She was in bed surrounded by her parents and sisters. Rallying a little when her mother called out my name, Kim smiled with her lopsided grin and said,

"Hey, Meina."

We had nothing more to say to each other that had not already been said.

Kim died a few days later.

That fall, when my husband and I returned to our winter home in Phoenix, we were shocked to see a tree that had grown three feet tall in our backyard in the exact spot where Kim had posed for photos during her visit. We had not planted this tree—nor had anyone else. It was as if Kim were sending a message to us that she remains with us in spirit and all is well. In 2016, at the writing of this book, the tree now stands 20 feet tall. We love to share the story of how it came to be in our backyard and about the young woman who bravely met life's challenges. Her life lesson to me was not to fear the unknown.

Of all the patients that I have cared for in my many years of nursing, I only danced, so to speak, on the floors of these two families. I often think about the coincidences connecting me with Taunya and Kim. Both young women were diagnosed and treated for the same type of tumors. Coincidentally they lived only ten minutes from each other, an hour and a half outside Calgary. Out of all the nurses on our unit, I cared for both of them. Both their families had sold their original homes and had purchased smaller properties, allowing Taunya's husband, Phil, and Kim's mother, Karen, to stay home and give the needed care. Kim died on the same unit where Taunya died. In fact, a beautiful fish tank purchased in memory of Taunya bubbled soothingly down the hall from Kim's room.

I often think about the complete love and commitment their families expressed among each other. My experience really knowing them all beyond the four walls of a hospital had me see what their lives were really about. They unselfishly shared their secrets, fears, and life lessons so I could grow as a more compassionate and understanding human being. If they hadn't asked and I hadn't chosen to be more than their nurse, I could have saved myself from years of tears and sadness. But by becoming personally involved with these two courageous women, my compassion as a nurse increased. I stayed connected to Kim and Taunya's families after their death. The memories of these two brave young women remain vivid and alive.

QUESTIONS TO ASK YOURSELF

1. What do you say to a patient who begins to cry with sadness or frustration?

2. Is it easy for you to relate with your patients in spite of their age and circumstances? Why or why not?

3. Could you see yourself accompanying a patient and her family on a trip?

CHAPTER 12

FAMILY AND FRIENDS CAN HEAL AND MOVE ON

What though the radiance which was once so bright
Be now forever taken from my sight,
  Though nothing can bring back the hour
Of splendor in the grass, of glory in the flower;
  We will grieve not, rather find
  Strength in what remains behind;

—*William Wordsworth*

AFTER READING THIS CHAPTER

You will examine your own concerns for the surviving family members and empower yourself with the knowledge that they will move on.

You will recognize that you do not always have to contain your humor.

THE PATIENT I NEVER FORGOT

After Flo died, I spent years thinking about this young mother of an adorable little toddler and wife to a devoted husband. A sarcoma made it necessary for Flo to have her left leg removed and too soon afterwards, she was a patient on our palliative unit. I will never forget her story.

I found it heartbreaking watching her husband come in every day, holding his little two-year-old boy's hand as they entered his wife's room. The child was too young to understand what was happening; he was just happy to see his mommy. His daddy would lift him up on the bed in the exact spot where Flo's leg used to be. Regardless of how she felt, Flo's face brightened up whenever she saw her little boy. Somehow, she found enough energy to play little games and cuddle with him.

At the end of their visit, his daddy would tell his son to say goodbye to his mommy. Then his daddy lifted him off the bed and out of the room. Always turning around before he walked out the door, the little boy would give his mommy a wave.

Toward the end of Flo's life, her husband came in alone to see her. Flo could no longer sense if her little boy was near her or not. Her husband would sit quietly by her bedside, holding her hand and whispering words of comfort that he trusted she could hear.

As her nurses, we found it difficult to watch her husband leave the unit for the last time, carrying Flo's few possessions with him as he quietly thanked us for our care. We could say few words other than "We're very sorry for your loss. Please take care of yourself and your little boy." As we watched the elevator door close and gave a final wave goodbye, my colleagues and I spent the next few minutes sharing our thoughts. Flo's death affected us, too, not only as nurses, but also as mothers. We felt a mutual sadness thinking about how Flo's husband would now be both mother and father to his son.

The thought of dying and leaving my children motherless was always a personal fear of mine. I would often think of Flo's husband and son, sending up a silent prayer and trusting that together, they were managing to get through the dark despair of loss with as much strength as possible. Ten years later, I was serving on a conference committee and recognized Flo's husband immediately as he came to the counter to see if he could help me with the signs I needed to have made for the symposium. He hadn't changed at all. After he finished helping me with the signs, I shared with him that I remembered him and his little boy when I had taken care of his wife in the hospital. I also told him that I often thought of the impact that Flo and her little family had on me.

"I apologized if I've caused you any upset by bringing up Flo's name," I said. "I just want you to know that she had not been forgotten by one of her many caregivers.

"Thank you," he said. "I'm grateful to know that you still remember Flo with fondness."

While speaking to him, I noticed he wore a wedding band on his left hand, silently happy and hopeful that he had managed to move on and find love once more. Only a month later, I noticed one of the therapists at the Cancer Centre shared the same last name as Flo.

"Are you related to Flo?" I asked.

Laughing, she said, "I'm actually married to Flo's husband!"

Laurel was one of the kindest and loveliest coworkers I have ever had the privilege to work with. Not only had she married Flo's husband, but she had been a friend of Flo's as well. Together, they were raising his son and her daughter. With that, I realized, yet again, that new opportunities could come from even the saddest situations. At the time of a great loss, loved ones often can't even imagine a brighter future because they are understandably stricken with grief. As nurses, though, we can hold the space of hope and new opportunities for our patients' grieving family members, trusting that they will find joy in life again.

QUESTIONS TO ASK YOURSELF

1. What support could you offer a patient, knowing she was going to die?

2. How could you support the surviving spouse of a patient as he or she leaves every day?

3. What might you say to him or her when his spouse dies?

THE HOMECOMING KING AND QUEEN

When I met Adam and his wife Linda, he was undergoing radiation treatments for a metastasized cancer. Reading his chart, I saw that he was my age and immediately felt a connection with him. Then I thought, "This could be my husband!"

I went to introduce myself to my new patient. Adam was lying on a stretcher with his wife standing beside him holding his hand. This couple should have been planning their retirement and future vacations, as my husband and I were doing. Instead, they were making funeral arrangements and decisions about Code Status and Personal Directives.

As an inpatient on our palliative care unit, Adam would be coming down to us for his five daily treatments. On his third treatment day, I asked Adam and his wife where they grew up. We realized we had all attended the same high school together—at the same time! They had even been the Prom King and Queen. Did I not remember? Then we shared a laugh as they admitted they were joking about being the King and Queen.

Even during this dark time, Adam and Linda were still able to joke and laugh. I was impressed that they spoke about the short future they had left together in such an easy and matter-of-fact manner. "Every day was a gift," they told me, and they had no regrets or anger that their remaining time was shorter than they had planned. They had just found out they were going to be grandparents and were elated with this news. Even though they knew Adam would not be around to meet this new little one, it did not dampen their excitement. They talked about how their daughter was feeling, what the name of the baby could be, and whether it would be a boy or a girl. They were seeing a positive future, even though Adam would not be part of it.

After finishing his treatments, Adam remained under our care while staying in the nursing unit upstairs and being treated for pain management. I continued to see him daily and kept updated about his progress. During one of our visits, Linda and I left Adam resting in bed to go chat together in a lounge room across the hall.

"I can't imagine living a life without Adam," she said. "All our dreams of growing old together, vacations, enjoying grandchildren look different for me now."

Then Linda told me she had made a promise to Adam to scatter his ashes on the St. Andrews golf course in Scotland.

"How will I do this without being arrested?" she asked me. We looked at each other and at the same time burst into laughter. Quickly getting control of ourselves, we tried continuing what had started off a serious conversation, but then moments later, we became hilarious again as we wiped tears of laughter from our eyes.

"Who would bail me out if I got caught?" she asked me with a grin. "How would I distribute an even amount of ashes in each hole and make sure I don't run out?"

We laughed uncontrollably as we imagined Linda being arrested for putting Adam's ashes in her pant cuffs. Then we tried to stifle our giggles. After all, we were on a palliative care unit, and laughter was not something you heard very often.

For a moment, we both forgot the seriousness of Linda's situation, briefly relieving her sadness with our laughter. Although most of the moments palliative care nurses share with our patients can be quite grave, I believe it's valuable for patients and their family members to remember how to laugh, adding light to moments of darkness.

Adam and Linda were wonderful teachers, not only to their family, but to me as well. They were open and accepting about Adam's situation. Despite his imminent passing, this powerfully connected couple could still make plans about what mattered to them. Every day they deepened their connection with one another, listening intently to what the other had to say because although Adam would not be physically part of their future together, he could still be involved in planning it. Linda freely expressed her fears about living alone since she had been with Adam as a teenager. The idea of living without him was difficult for her to accept. Adam reassured her that she was strong.

"You'll be able to carry on," he assured her.

Linda shared their conversations with me, and although I could not possibly know what she was going through, I could support her by listening to her fears. Several months after Adam died, I received a note from Linda telling me they were not only expecting one grandchild, but four! Both their son and daughter were having twins!

QUESTIONS TO ASK YOURSELF

1. How easy is it for you to see a positive aspect, even in a tragedy?

2. A patient asks you, "What would you do, if you were in my position?" Do you tell them honestly what you would do, or would you tell them what you think they want to hear and why?

3. Is it difficult or easy for you to use appropriate humor, even in a sad situation?

PART II

OPTIMIZING YOUR OWN SELF-CARE AND THE CARE YOU GIVE YOUR PATIENTS

In the end, only three things matter
How much you loved
How gently you loved
How gracefully you let go
of things not meant for you.

— *Buddha*

CHAPTER 13

PREPARING FOR THE MANY RESPONSES TO TERMINAL ILLNESS

There are as many responses as there are situations surrounding death. You do not need to take them personally.

AFTER READING THIS CHAPTER

You will evaluate your own experience and feelings towards death.

You will acknowledge a patient and family's situation with empathy.

RESPONDING TO DEATH'S KNOCK

Death is inevitable for all of us. However, death is not a subject we ordinarily feel comfortable talking about. The majority of us file it into a "someday" category. Those who have had someone close to them die may have questions, thoughts, and feelings that influence their ideas about their own death: "Will my death be painful?" "Will I die alone?" "What happens to me after I die?" "What happens to them?" Such questions can cause apprehension or a sense of foreboding, making it easier not to think about death at all. Don't most of us live in the world of "It's not going to happen today"?

Perhaps you have not had the experience of a loved one dying, so death may not be a part of life you are personally familiar with. Your knowledge about death may be only through someone else's journey, or perhaps from what you have read. Beginning a career caring for patients who have heard death's knock may make you feel uncomfortable about establishing a relationship with them. Caring for and about someone who is dying doesn't necessarily become easier, but by employing the principles described in this book, over the course of your career you will learn to trust your intuition when responding to the needs of your patients and their families. Each person and each family is different. Connection is the key. Be yourself. Remember why you went into nursing in the first place and the commitment you made. Your own motives for becoming a nurse will shine through as you care for your patients. Keep asking yourself one fundamental question: "How would I want my family member to be attended to?" This question can be a powerful place to begin your journey as a palliative care nurse.

When someone receives a diagnosis of a terminal illness and hears Death's knock, he or she may experience shock, numbness, and fear. After all, Death is an unwelcome, uninvited and untimely guest who has shown up unannounced. Your patient's response may be, "Not now. This isn't the right time," or "I'm not ready to die. I'm not finished living yet," or even, "This isn't fair. Why me?"

We are all powerless to ask Death to return another day. This intruder determines when he comes, regardless of how old we are or what we're currently up to in our life. Death can claim anyone with or without notice, regardless of age.

With a terminal diagnosis, patients and their families will become well aware of how short life really is. Their bucket list may not be completed yet, or they may not even have written it. The direction of their thoughts must now turn from everyday routines and future plans to applications for long term disability, insurance forms, last wills and testaments, and personal directives. Final goodbyes become paramount. Old feuds may now either rise up or seem trivial. Forgiveness and making peace with family and friends may become paramount. This definitive awareness of a person's life coming to a close can often leave your patients and their family members feeling emotionally out of control.

This is why you, as a healthcare professional, may see patients or their loved ones display anger and frustration. Their anger may even be focused straight at you. Since you are in the direct line of fire, it's not unusual to find yourself the target of their outrage. It can be difficult not to take their anger personally. Knowing that you, a relative stranger, are simply an easier mark than pointing the anger at themselves—or the people they know and love—can make their actions toward you more understandable.

Families may snap at you to go get their loved one an apple juice: "And do it now!" They may become clock watchers, looking anxiously down the hallway, waiting for you. You will be attempting to give excellent care to your patient and ensure they are comfortable. But, in the family's eyes, you don't seem to be doing enough, doing it correctly, or doing it quickly. As a new nurse, I often felt the need to defend myself, telling the family or friends of my patients about my workload: "I haven't even had a break yet, and it's already 2:00 in the afternoon!" But, of course, families don't care about that. Their loved one is facing death. Their loved one's comfort is their first concern. As nurses, our personal needs, as well as the needs of other patients we are attending to, are not a family's concern.

Perhaps the family's frustration and displeasure is misdirected because they feel guilty about not spending enough time with their loved one in the past. They may be overcompensating to make sure that nurses and physicians are doing everything they themselves did not provide in the past or cannot provide in the present for their family member. This hyper-vigilance of family members can make them feel less guilty about the lack of support they may not have given before. In addition, your patient may be directing his or her own anger at loved ones, and in turn, the loved ones direct it at you. Sitting with someone you love who is in pain, watching the clock for the next scheduled dose of analgesia, can be stressful and taxing: "It's been 4 hours and 10 minutes since his last pain medication! It was due 10 minutes ago!"

As a nurse, if you're late delivering pain medication, bringing it to your attention can make family members feel they are somehow giving more support to their loved one. The family may feel that reprimanding you or hurrying you along is at least something they can do. Families will often say or do anything to make sure you're giving their loved one the best care possible.

Relating to the feelings your patient or their family members are experiencing helps minimize the impact on you as a nurse. Spending even a moment acknowledging that it must be difficult for them, and asking if there is anything they need, can show family members that you're working with them and not against them. A simple gesture such as offering a warm blanket for their comfort can assure them that you appreciate their support and presence. To alleviate the anxiety of responsibility they might be feeling, keep encouraging them to call if they require anything or have questions.

When patients or family members react angrily toward you, or even toward each other, it helps to realize that anger is a secondary emotion covering up their primary feelings of sadness or fear. Dr. Thomas Gordon, an American Clinical Psychologist widely recognized as a pioneer in teaching communication skills and conflict resolution, explains that hurt, rejection, insecurity, or pain could be other secondary emotions igniting people's anger under stress.[1]

A patient's loved ones may be feeling a lack of control within themselves, so along with anger, they may feel guilt and pain about the past or about not being able to do enough to relieve any suffering their loved one might be experiencing. Patients and families often look to you, the nurse on duty, as a representative of the medical system, which may have let them down in the past with a misdiagnosis or a delay in treatment. If they see the system as having failed to give your patient the support needed, families may find it easier to direct anger toward you, a nurse who represents what is otherwise a faceless system. At times, it may feel as though there are not enough minutes in the day to do all your assigned duties. By taking a minute without being summoned to stop and see how your patient is doing, you can help minimize many of a family's concerns. Assessing your patient's response to the last dose of analgesia can add a level of assurance for the family that you're being diligent in your care. When your patient and his or her family connects with you as someone who is on their side and there to support them, you will notice their anxiety minimize, which will reduce your own stress levels. You may also even notice that your patient's call bell doesn't ring as often.

I recall a particular patient and her family who never seemed satisfied with any of the nursing care I or any other nurse gave. Every time the call bell rang for this room, I cringed.

"What now?" I would mutter under my breath.

I began to hate the sound of my name on the overhead page as I was summoned to this patient's room again and again. Sharing my frustration with my co-workers gave me only temporary relief. I realized that I could not change the way the patient or her family were behaving, but I could change my response to them and the situation.

I decided to play a little mind game with myself called, "First Time." Whenever her call bell rang, I would answer it as though I had never been summoned before. I would enter the room with the same attitude as if it were a new experience. Playing the "First Time" game caused a shift in me. I no longer felt the frustrating dread of having to go in and see what was wanted "now." After all, it was just the first time my patient or her family had called. I know they did not change, but my view of them altered. There was no past history of discouraging conversations or demands. I felt newness, and along with that, a refreshed commitment to deliver my care.

Families and patients will respond very differently to the care that you give. One family cannot thank you enough. They'll send you wordy cards, flowers, and treats with your name on it. Another family can storm off the unit, fuming about a lack of support and may even lodge a complaint or lawsuit. Accept and enjoy the gratitude you receive from your patients and their families. Their gratitude validates the reason you chose this profession. Anything less (ingratitude, impatience, misdirected fury) interferes with your personal well-being and adds to your own level of stress. Let go of any negative energy as quickly as possible. You will empower your life with balance, peace, and satisfaction that you chose a career in nursing.

On a, less than perfect day, you can remember that another perfect day is just around the corner.

QUESTIONS TO ASK YOURSELF

1. What has been your experience with death?

2. Have your experiences, or lack of experience, impacted your outlook about your own death?

3. How could you respond to an angry family member knowing their anger is likely a secondary emotion?

CHAPTER 14

SEEKING ONGOING SUPPORT FROM OTHER NURSES

You may be working alongside
your greatest support system.

AFTER READING THIS CHAPTER

You will recognize the resources
at hand when needed.

You will empower your own coping mechanisms.

EMPOWERING PATIENTS WITH ANSWERS

Nurses often share their frustrations with coworkers because we provide each other with a safe space to unload and speak and have our experiences be understood. You know you are doing your best, but venting to someone who has walked in your shoes can restore your confidence and motivation, as well as renew your energy and commitment.

A quick hug of understanding from your co-worker is sometimes all you need to continue on with your day. It is perfectly ok to ask for the hug as well. "Mary, I am feeling very frustrated with the family in Room 620 right now. Can I just get a quick hug of encouragement?" Not only do you feel the support from Mary, you have given Mary permission to ask you for support if she needs it.

Try finding another nurse or supervisor who may have a few moments to support you by letting you talk through your experience and your emotions. This person can help you calm down and can also suggest possible solutions. Sometimes, just talking briefly to someone who empathizes and will listen to you can make all the difference in the moment. Holding on to negative thoughts will not only deplete your energy but rob you of your focus, which may lead to errors in calculations. Negative thoughts and feelings can build up, spilling out later when you misdirect frustration, impatience, or anger toward your patients, another co-worker, your family, friends, or even yourself. It is important to be aware of any potential signs that obscure your optimal self.

Once you regain your composure and have time to reflect on the incident, look at what happened. Is there an opportunity for you to learn from this event? Can others learn from your experience?

As senior nurses, we have witnessed, over the years, the heartbreak of watching our co-workers struggle with fatigue, depression, addiction, and even being forced to leave the vocation they once loved and were committed to because hospital administrators in the past offered little support and little time off. In fact, taking time off was actually frowned upon and showed a sign of weakness. Today's administrators recognize the need to support their front-line staff. If staff members are not working at their optimal level, not only do we as nurses struggle, but patient care is ultimately affected.

Many nurses arrive on shift after having worked hours already to organize their personal lives first. You may, for example, have delivered your children to child care after ensuring their homework has been done and lunches made. You may also have made dinner for your family because they'll arrive home hours before your shift is over. Being given a patient assignment that takes all of your self-control and patience for the next twelve hours will only add to your fatigue. Balancing your career responsibilities with your responsibilities at home is not always an easy task. When assessing your household requirements, give yourself permission to focus on what needs to be done and leave less important tasks for your days off. Also, ask other nurses what they do in order to have their personal and professional lives work.

Today, you need to be equipped with information about the signs and symptoms of potential threats that challenge your overall well-being. Supporting one another with encouragement and understanding will not only help nurses who may be struggling, but can also be powerful in preventing future episodes of distress and burn out that we see commonly in our line of work.

Nanette Wiser wrote an article in the AMN Healthcare log "Nursing Stress Can Lead to High Divorce Rates," stating that in 2016, the divorce rate for nurses was higher than for doctors and other professions, especially among women. Ms. Wiser quoted University of Minnesota professor William Doherty, "Two-thirds of divorces are initiated by women." He also states nursing ranks in the top ten professions most likely to divorce.

These are sobering statistics and no doubt managing a career and family on your own would escalate stress levels considerably.

QUESTIONS TO ASK YOURSELF

1. Do your peers provide a safe environment to unload your frustrations?

2. How might you encourage the sharing of feelings with your co-workers?

3. Do you develop close relationships with your peers outside of your work?

CHAPTER 15

DEVELOPING YOUR SELF-CARE COMMITMENT PLAN

You cannot support others
if your own resources are depleted.

AFTER READING THIS CHAPTER

You will develop your own self-care plan.

You will recognize the importance of self-care.

YOU ARE A GIFT TO YOUR PATIENTS

Developing a Self-Care Commitment Plan will help you discover and commit to practicing what serves and nurtures you in a powerful way. Taking care of yourself first so that you can care for others may feel selfish sometimes, but self-care is imperative for anyone working in healthcare. You must maintain your own health, so you can help your patients with theirs. Think of taking care of yourself as no different from the instructions we receive when a flight attendant prepares us for handling an airplane emergency: "Put on your own oxygen mask first before assisting others."

The care you provide to those who are dying can slowly chip away at your endurance. Palliative care nurses perform physically challenging and emotionally draining work. Admitting that you need support is not admitting failure. Acknowledge that you must be vigilant about your own health, and get support whenever you feel your resources are being depleted. Ensuring you perform within your full capability is just as important as ensuring your patients are receiving everything they need to be comfortable. Sometimes as a nurse you focus so much on the needs of everyone around you that you forget, or even believe it is not right, to shine the spotlight on yourself. Your own health matters. If you ignore your own physical and emotional needs, your patients, your family, and you, yourself, will suffer needlessly.

Benjamin Franklin's advice that "An ounce of prevention is worth a pound of cure" fits well with developing a Self-Care Commitment Plan for anyone in the medical profession. Although he was speaking of fire prevention, the quote is often used referring to health.[2]

A proactive care plan would be ideal, but when we are feeling our best, we do not necessarily put self-care as a priority. It is not until we experience mental or physical exhaustion that we realize our own wellbeing is necessary to carry on.

I have found there is no shut off valve that I can use at the end of my day. Various scenarios of the day replay in my mind repeatedly. An 8-hour shift can often become a 14-plus-hour emotional work load. Developing my own Self-Care Commitment plan made me aware of the importance of placing my needs first. I knew that as important as my role as a nurse was, in order to continue I would have to take on my own wellbeing no differently than taking care of the wellbeing of my patients.

My own Self-Care Commitment Plan consists of eight goals. When I first wrote down my self-care goals, I began by focusing on what my body and mind needed. When are the times I feel at peace, calm and good about myself? As the thoughts came to me I wrote them down. In a perfect world, I would be meeting these eight goals all the time. But when I don't meet my self-care goals, I forgive myself for not being flawless. What is important is to have some plan for reviewing goals at least once a month and recommitting to them or making adjustments as needed. I pick the 30th of the month to review my goals because it's the date of my birth and easy to remember. I place a reminder on my calendar to alert me.

MY SELF-CARE COMMITMENT PLAN

1. **Sleep** - Ensure I get an adequate amount of sleep and the rest my body requires. At this stage of my life, that means at least 8 hours of sleep a night. Current research by the National Sleep Foundation recommends 7 to 9 hours of sleep for an adult between 18 and 64 years of age. I also avoid certain stimulants, such as coffee before bedtime or a dramatic movie, which will interfere with the quality of my sleep.

2. **Eat Healthy** - Prepare foods that support my body to do what it is meant to do. Limit carbs and fats and eat adequate amounts of protein, fruits, and vegetables. Health Canada's Food Guide has supportive guidelines for nutrition as well as exercise. I have found planning and making my lunches for work the night before prevents me making unhealthy choices at work, when I have had no time to prepare it in the morning.

3. **Exercise** - Do cardio and strength building to protect my body from wear and tear, especially since I spend most of my day on my feet and assisting patients physically. The older I get, the better my excuses also get for not participating in a regular exercise program. For me, walking works best as a weight-bearing exercise. During my walks, I can meditate, plan, and de-stress. When finished, I feel quite energized. I also keep a set of weights in view of my television so that even when watching a program, I can lift a set of weights easily.

4. **Balance** - Make time for things I enjoy: writing, reading, socializing with friends, and spending time with family. Sitting on my deck with a good novel and escaping into an author's printed world is one of my favorite energizing activities. Visiting friends provides lightness and laughter—and a welcome change from work days filled with sadness and death. It also grounds me with gratitude. I found a powerful article on 3.Wikipedia.org about Work-family conflict that looks at our jobs interfering with our personal time as well as our personal time interrupting our work time and

the stress it can cause. For instance, missing work to tend to a sick child and knowing that your peers are now working short staffed can add a layer of conflict and feeling torn as to where our commitment lies.

5. **Mindfulness** - Begin my day with meditation and prayer. Even when a busy day lies ahead, by waking up 15 minutes earlier and spending a short time in the quiet and stillness, I feel more grounded. Susan Kuchinskas quotes Charles L. Raison, NC clinical director of the Mind-Body Program at Emory University School of Medicine: "Those who meditate can choose among a wide range of practices, both religious and secular. What they have in common are a narrowing of focus that shuts out the external world and usually a stilling of the body."[3] On my days off I begin my day with 30-60 minutes of meditation.

6. **Journal** – Write a few words in my journal before I go to sleep. It sits next to my bedside table so I don't forget. Being grateful and acknowledging your blessings bring abundance into your life. Amy Morin, psychotherapist and contributing editor to a November 2014 *Forbes* article, writes in her article "Seven Scientifically Proven Benefits of Gratitude that will Motivate you to Give Thanks Year-Round" that journaling your gratitude will open the doors for improved relationships, improve physical and psychological health, enhance empathy and reduce regression, help you sleep better, improve your self-esteem, and increase your mental strength.[4]

7. **Intentions** - Set an intention for the day such as, "Today I will be a powerful listener" or "Today I will be connected with other people." After setting an intention, I remind myself during the day who I have promised myself to be. Setting intentions helps me stay grounded and empowers me to fulfill my commitment to listen, connect, or be forgiving. Deepak Chopra, MD states in "The 7 Spiritual Laws of Success": "An intention is a directed impulse of consciousness that contains the seed for that which you aim to create."[5]

8. **Change Unhealthy Habits** - Be aware of the times I want to numb myself with alcohol or unhealthy food. When I reflect on my thoughts at the time and what would have me want to over indulge, I realize these

are usually the same thoughts that can keep me from exercising: "This is too hard," "It's not that important," "I deserve this." My ego would like to escape from reality and find an easier way out. I deal with these very human thoughts by forgiving myself and starting fresh. I recommit to my healthy eating habits and to what I want in my life. I do not dwell on my failures and drag them with me. By being responsible for my thoughts and my own health, I can have honest conversations with my patients. After all, how can I invite them to live a healthier life style when they look at me and see someone who is obviously not walking the talk? I tell them it's not always an easy journey. I share with them that I struggle as well. I don't pretend to have my life in perfect order. I am a human being, capable of making mistakes and experiencing struggles just like they are. I'm not afraid to show my patients this part of me, while also sharing with them my commitment to living a healthy life.

These are the eight goals that make up my own Self–Care Commitment Plan. I challenge you to write out your own self-care plan. Track your progress and the goals you've achieved using the Self-Care Commitment Plan Template you can download from my website: www.MeinaDubetz.com/commitment-plan.

For additional support, consider creating your Self-Care Commitment Plan with another nurse you trust and with whom you share a similar goal. During one of your breaks, invite him or her to talk with you about your self-care commitments and ask her if she'd be willing to write one of her own. Then review it together once a month on the same day and at the same time, so you can hold each other accountable, supporting one another in the commitments you are now making and meeting for yourself.

How to Keep Yourself Empowered All Day

In addition to taking care of yourself over the long term by writing a Self-Care Commitment Plan, you will want a plan for coping with the daily challenges of being a nurse. There may be moments when you will feel overwhelmed. You might get triggered by an event or by what someone says to you, your patient, or a co-worker. At that moment, you no longer feel in control of your emotions. Holding it together until you get home seems hours away.

If one of your peers or supervisor is not available to listen, my second suggestion is to empower yourself in the moment. Waiting until you have a break may be too long, and waiting until someone is available to support you will not help you in the moment. The minute you're feeling upset, angry, or out of control use the following five tips to regain your composure:

FIVE TIPS TO CALM YOURSELF AT ANY MOMENT: "S T A R T"

1. **Step away** from where you're physically standing. I find walking to the nearest utility room or even a washroom works well.

2. **Take purposeful breaths** in and out three times slowly. Pay attention to your breaths. Imagine the air coming in through the soles of your feet and traveling up through your body until it reaches the top of your head. Hold your breath for a couple of seconds and slowly release it. Feel your breath move down through your body and out the soles of your feet.

3. **Assess** what you are thinking and how you are interpreting it. Is there an underlying issue? Your feeling upset may actually be related to your vacation being cancelled, your unreliable childcare, or a strained relationship with your spouse, partner, or person you're dating. Sometimes recognizing what is actually upsetting you can help you calm down in the moment and find a solution to the actual problem away from work.

4. **Realize** that you are not alone. There are others willing to support you.

5. **Tell** yourself this is only a moment in time. Your life will not be defined by it, nor should your day.

QUESTIONS TO ASK YOURSELF

1. Develop your own self-care module.

2. Do you have any other tools that could assist you in de-stressing in the moment? If not, could the "Five Steps to Calm Yourself at Any Moment" work for you?

3. What do you do to ensure balance between your personal and professional life as a nurse?

CHAPTER 16

TAKING CARE OF YOUR OWN SAFETY UNDER DANGEROUS SITUATIONS

Even the calmest environment can become volatile in a moment's notice.

AFTER READING THIS CHAPTER

You will understand the importance of self-protection.

You will become aware of your workplace support system in volatile situations.

YOU ARE #1

I have always found the following Buddhist advice powerful: "No one saves us but ourselves. No one can and no one may. We ourselves must walk the path." As a nurse, you must be responsible to take care of your own safety.

When your patient's family members become stressed, they commonly release their anger and frustration in the presence of their loved one, whom they believe to be sleeping or unaware. Regardless of a person's condition, medical personnel have always assumed that patients can still be affected by sounds or conversations around them. It is good practice to ask loved ones to continue any escalated discussions outside your patient's room. Simply motion toward your patient and suggest their discussion take place in a different location, so as to not disturb their loved one. Often when upset, the person speaking does not even realize that voices are becoming louder. Mentioning a change of location brings an awareness to the escalated conversation and may give them a few moments to become calmer as they move to another place. When you empathize with what they are saying, you may help them regain their composure. Listening to them express their distress, anger, or frustration does not mean that you have to agree with what they are saying. You are merely a sounding board for them to get their thoughts into dialogue.

Evaluate the level of frustration and anger. At times, the elevated discussion is best held in a private room. Assess, too, if this problem is one that you can manage on your own. Is the unit supervisor or the patient's physician the best one to be involved in the discussion? If the family's concern is about you personally, ensure you are not subjected to verbal or possible physical abuse.

When it comes to your patient or a family member expressing anger, sometimes your explanations or empathetic phrases can still escalate the situation and even lead into violence. I cannot emphasize enough that your safety is of the utmost importance. Many hospitals have an overhead code system for a violent situation. Security personnel come immediately to assist and stabilize a volatile environment. Smaller institutions may not have the luxury of adequate security personnel. Do not try to reassure or reason with an enraged or out-of-control person. In such cases, you and your colleagues should call the local police for support.

Some years ago, the oncology unit I worked on admitted a patient with dementia. Our nursing staff was surprised and distressed at the inappropriateness of admitting this person. We were an oncology unit and not equipped with the training to care for this patient's anger and out-of-control behavior. But the medical and psychiatric units had no available beds. Tragically, this man managed to injure three nurses in a single day. After he pushed one nurse against the wall, she had to have shoulder surgery; another nurse had to take time off work for a short time to recover from bruises he caused by hitting her when she came to the aid of her co-worker.

It was the third nurse's injury that led to a heart-breaking ending. Our patient's attack on her resulted in a serious back injury. She was on long-term disability for more than a year, spending her days filled with endless physiotherapy appointments, doctors' appointments, counseling appointments and reams of paperwork for workman's compensation. To control her pain, she took long and short acting morphine. At times, the pain was so severe she needed to increase her analgesia, which would then prevent her from driving or interacting with others. It became obvious that she would not be returning to active nursing—the work she loved. She then focused on obtaining her master's degree, hoping to teach one day, but after taking a few classes realized teaching would not give her the personal fulfillment that bedside nursing had given her. Dealing with her broken dreams and the unrelieved pain became too unmanageable. One day, she drove up to the mountains and ended her suffering by ending her life.

Perhaps the tragic case of the third nurse seems extreme, but a study of Post-Traumatic Stress Disorder (PTSD) completed in February 2016 in Manitoba, Canada by the Manitoba Nurses Union identified five scenarios that lead to PTSD in nurses. Not surprisingly, violence is number two.[6]

FIVE LEADING CAUSES OF POST-TRAUMATIC STRESS DISORDER IN NURSES

1. Death of a child, particularly due to abuse.
2. Violence at work.
3. Treating patients that resemble family or friends.
4. Death of a patient or injury to a patient after undertaking extraordinary efforts to save a life.
5. Heavy patient loads.

QUESTIONS TO ASK YOURSELF

1. What support is available at your Institution to provide staff protection against violence?

2. What support could you give the family of your aggressive patient?

3. What could you do to de-escalate a potentially violent situation?

CHAPTER 17

ANSWERING YOUR PATIENT'S DIFFICULT QUESTIONS

Honesty matters, even if that means admitting you do not know the answer.

AFTER READING THIS CHAPTER

The reader will acknowledge and support her patient's difficult questions.

The reader will ensure that the patient has contact of available resources of support.

DIFFICULT CONVERSATIONS

After a doctor has given his patient a prognosis, it's not unusual for the patient to ask, "How long do I have left to live?" Some physicians will give statistics and averages but avoid answering the question directly. I've observed that most patients want information directly related to them and not average life spans derived from clinical research. You may find once the physician leaves the room, your patient will turn to you and ask, "How long do I really have to live? What do *you* think?"

I have no magic crystal ball with just the right answer, even after 30 years as a nurse. If you feel comfortable and confident understanding what the physician has told them, you might begin the conversation with asking the patient what she understood her doctor to say. If further clarification is needed, then you may start by saying, "It sounded to me like your doctor was speaking of weeks instead of months" or "months instead of a year." What you say also depends on where your patient is on his or her journey. Is she still receiving treatments? If so, I tell my patients that everyone is an individual when it comes to how they respond to their treatments. Determining a time frame would be more accurate after their treatments are completed and they return for a follow-up appointment. Try to take your patients' focus off when they are going to die; instead encourage them to focus on actively getting support while they're living.

I am fortunate to work with some physicians who take the patient's question about how long they have to live as an important piece of the treatment plan and care they give. These physicians have developed a comfortable relationship with death; they do not appear to fear this serious conversation with their patients. Unfortunately, there are still some doctors who quote statistics and averages in order to avoid answering a patient's question directly. It is not your responsibility as a nurse to answer this important patient question. You may even need to ask the patient's doctor to speak to his or her patient again.

Not long ago I was in a room with a physician and a patient asked the doctor, "How long do you think I have left to live?" The physician took the palm of his right hand and slapped it on his own forehead, saying "I was hoping you wouldn't ask me that!" While speaking, he rolled his eyes upward and spun his revolving stool away from the patient. This doctor's lighthearted and insensitive response to a patient's sincere question stunned me. If his words were not inconsiderate enough, slapping his palm on his forehead as he twirled back in his chair, acting like it was the last thing he wanted to deal with, was totally inappropriate. It must have taken courage for this patient to ask about her own mortality. Maybe his own discomfort with death and his inability to relate to his patient's emotional needs caused the doctor to joke about a very serious question.

I felt embarrassed and wanted nothing else but to go and soothe my shocked patient. I waited for the physician to acknowledge or apologize, but I soon realized that would not be happening. I suspected this physician wanted to avoid giving his patient a direct response because it was such hopeless news. Then, in an effort to offer some type of response, the physician began rambling off statistics and averages, perhaps hoping the patient would figure out a timeline herself. Instead, the young woman had stopped listening and didn't acknowledge the doctor's information. No doubt, she was still thunderstruck with the physician's first unprofessional response.

When patients hear a new diagnosis or the upsetting news that their treatments are no longer effective, they will usually need time to have this information become real for them. It's difficult to absorb such shocking news, and questions often come later.

In an outpatient setting, ensure your patient has a contact number to call with any further questions. Depending on the circumstances, you may want to call the patient yourself if you know he or she is waiting to hear about a treatment plan decision, or if you feel the need to check up on them. Jotting a note in your calendar as a reminder for yourself to call will keep you connected to your patients' needs.

If the patient is in hospital, ensuring documentation is available for other health care members of the information that the patient has previously received will maintain and continue support for the patient between caregivers.

Patients may be coping with other stressors in their lives. Receiving news of a terminal diagnosis, failed treatment, or a short amount of time left to live will add to their inability to cope. Making yourself aware of what your patient is presently struggling with will give you a better indication of how to fully support them. I have often seen elderly patients receive a terminal diagnosis and their main concern was not that they were dying, but that they were the main caregiver for a loved one at home. They may need support finding someone to take over their caregiver role. In this case, it's important to ensure home care is in place to support the family member in order to best support your patient.

Support groups provide invaluable connections for people dealing with similar life- threatening experiences. Speaking to someone who is going through a comparable process is sometimes easier then talking to a family member or friend. Your facility will offer contact numbers for your patient to call or display notices in common areas for patients and families to see. During my own experience after the death of my son, speaking to family, friends, and even a psychiatrist did very little to support me. As much as they wanted to help me, they had no idea what I was coping with. The only person who helped me through my journey was my cousin, who had suffered the same loss. She not only understood but could connect with my grief.

Your next meeting or phone call with your patient will have given them some time to adjust to the news they received. At this time, you can determine what path they wish to pursue. Are treatments an option? What are the patient's wishes? Is there a future event she wishes to attend? If that is not possible, could the event be moved up? Perhaps your patient could record or write a personal message if it is doubtful she will be able to attend. Does he need support with his choice to stop any further treatments? Is it okay for him to have his journey end at this time, or does he feel like that would be giving up?

In Chapter 5, I wrote about a gentleman who had been diagnosed with a Stage 4 brain tumor. His sister was with him during his appointments, and it was evident that my patient was agreeing to his radiation treatments because of his sister's views about what he needed, not his own. Patients do not want to hurt their family's feelings or appear as if they are giving up. Sometimes they will make a decision based on their family's wishes, not their own. Ask your patient the question, "What is important to you right now?" That can give your patient clarification, but most importantly, the permission to put into words what is on his mind and what he actually wants. I have asked a patient before what he would like to do and was astounded when he told me he was only continuing the treatments because he didn't want to disappoint his doctor, who was working so hard to keep him alive.

Another frequent question I hear from my patients following unwelcome news is, "Why me? I have always eaten a healthy diet and been active? Why would I get a terminal disease? It's not fair." These questions are reasonable, especially when they continue by saying they knew someone who smoked and drank but lived until she was in her late 80s. When patients respond this way, I acknowledge their frustrations. I also acknowledge them for having chosen a healthy life style. I tell them, "The fact that you have built up a strong body will support you as you receive treatments." Letting patients know that their healthy life style choices will actually aid them through their current journey can soften the unfairness they sometimes feel at having been given a life-threatening diagnosis in spite of doing everything "right."

"Why me?" questions are not limited to patients who have lived a healthy life style. An elderly patient may also be wondering why her life has to end with cancer. Why could she not just slip away during her sleep, which would be preferable to having daily chemotherapy and radiation treatment? Your patient could refuse treatments and allow nature to take its course, but refusing treatments does not necessarily make her journey any easier. Homecare support and palliative care will invade the privacy of her home. Arrangements for other accommodations may be necessary. What was once a peaceful and predictable life is now interrupted by strangers and unfamiliar routines.

Allowing patients to express their feelings and frustrations by giving them an understanding sympathetic ear is sometimes all they need. Patients will move through different stages of grief as you support them with your empathy. It is not uncommon for patients to feel despair or depression and to act upon those signs and symptoms. When a person lacks the desire to continue on with life, he or she will benefit from professional intervention. Encourage your patient to speak to a counselor to support him as he verbalizes his feelings. Telling your patient that seeing a counselor has benefited others who have experienced similar feelings. Validating feelings and emotions as normal can give your patient a sense of not being alone in this experience. You can also offer to make a phone call to set up counseling, because patients will rarely make a call like this for themselves. Initiating the call will ensure your patient gets the counseling support that he or she deserves and that can ease their difficult journey.

Regardless of the questions you have asked and the psychological screening forms your patient may have filled out, you may very well have a terminally ill patient who dies by suicide, despite your best efforts and support. Dr. Fang Fang of the Karolinska Institute of Stockholm led a 2012 study, with results published in the *New England Journal of Medicine*. The study shows that a patient will be 13 times more likely to commit suicide one week after receiving a terminal diagnosis. Of all the suicides, 10% of them will be related to receiving this life-altering news. A patient is six times more likely to die by myocardial infarction, a heart attack, one week following the same prognosis.[7]

With these statistics, it's easy to see the importance of assessing patients' mental well-being. Screening tools are sometimes used prior to their seeing a doctor. Inquiries related to physical side effects as well as screening for emotional coping abilities can alert you and the physician about any need to monitor an individual, ensuring your patient receives both the physical and emotional support he or she may need.

The forms patients fill out are designed for privacy so that patients can answer difficult questions more comfortably, rather than having them answer direct questions in front of family members. Your patient may feel a sense of protectiveness towards his family members, not wanting them to know what his true thoughts or symptoms are. Forms also allow you to be discreet about the questions you ask your patient. After reading a patient's form, you may choose to speak to your patient privately, depending on their answers.

As laws are changing with regard to Medical Assistance in Dying (MAID) or Death with Dignity, I also hear more patients asking for information about taking control of when and how they die. Regardless of your own opinions, your duty as a nurse is to ensure that you honor your patient's inquiries. The information your patient is requesting could be given by their physician or a referral to another medical provider for more concrete directions. Listening to your patients and allowing them to verbalize their thoughts in a safe, non-judgmental space is most important.

QUESTIONS TO ASK YOURSELF

1. Your patient has just been told he has a short time to live. What could you say to him?

2. Your patient abruptly leaves the room after being told disturbing news. What could you do? How would you follow up with her?

3. A patient has requested information on Medical Assistance in Dying (MAID) and this goes against your personal beliefs. Take a moment to think about how you can provide support to your patient and respect your own principles.

CHAPTER 18

YOU DON'T HAVE TO KNOW EVERYTHING TO PROVIDE QUALITY NURSING CARE

You do not have to know everything –
you just have to know where to find the answers.

AFTER READING THIS CHAPTER

You will recognize opportunities to enhance your abilities to give care.

You will assess your thoughts about asking for assistance when unsure of procedures.

STAGES OF GRIEF

If you think you need to have all the answers in order to be an effective nurse, you will soon become your own worst critic. When I completed my schooling, I thought I should have the knowledge to handle any medical situation. After all, I was a Registered Nurse and my patients would be depending on me for all of their needs.

As a new grad I walked into a patient's room filled with visitors. My knees were trembling as I put on my "I am capable" expression. I felt as if all their eyes were on me. I was the one who would be caring for their loved one, and they were making sure I was qualified. I introduced myself to my patient and then turned to the visitors, asking how they were related to the patient. I felt the atmosphere shift almost immediately as they told me how they were related: mother, father, sister, brother, husband, wife, and friend. I now felt a connection with them individually. We were no longer strangers. Our goal was the same—to ensure their loved one would receive the highest quality of care and attention she needed and deserved.

Don't be afraid to ask for support from more experienced nurses. The first few times I set up an infusion for a narcotic, I had another nurse come in to assist me and be my second set of eyes. There is no shame in having another nurse come into the room to assist with a task if you feel unsure of yourself. A simple explanation about a double check will reassure your patients and families. If I were a family member, I know I would feel uneasy watching a nurse attempting a task I could see she was unsure of, so get the support you need. If you are a new graduate nurse or a new hospice care worker, you may have limited experience speaking to patients about end-of-life situations. There is no manual available that can assist with every situation.

Elisabeth Kübler-Ross wrote a classic study in the 1960s *On Death and Dying.*[8] Her research describes the various stages patients may experience when confronted with an end-of-life diagnosis. Even though Kübler-Ross's book may seem dated, her research findings about the stages of grief remain unchanged and are still widely used today. I have added my own commentary after each of Kübler-Ross's brief definitions of each stage.

1. Denial *"The first reaction is denial. In this stage individuals believe the diagnosis is somehow mistaken, and cling to a false, preferable reality."*

I have been present in the room when a patient has received a grim prognosis. I find it difficult to watch the expressions on their faces reflecting their thoughts as they mentally digest the news they have just received. Before the doctor speaks, patients usually appear a little nervous, knowing that the news they are about to hear may change their planned future. They sometimes prolong the current conversation to put off hearing what the doctor is waiting to tell them. It is "safer" for them to remain in the present moment. They are aware as soon as their doctor begins to speak that their world will alter. The doctor delivers the news, and a visible pallor appears in their faces, as if any color has suddenly drained out. They appear numb, sometimes unable to speak. Their thoughts are working overtime, and they are unable to unscramble those thoughts in order to connect with what is happening right now. Then slowly the thoughts appear to move into disbelief; their eyes often fill with tears as they grasp the reality of what the doctor is saying. Some patients may take several minutes to reach this point of reality. Denial sets in moments later, in response to the mind's mission to protect a space of vulnerability to threat.

When I reflect upon the moment I was told about the death of my son, I went through the same process. My mind was saying, "It is not true. They are wrong. There is a mistake. I will show them and prove them wrong."

2. Anger *When the individual recognizes that denial cannot continue, they become frustrated, especially at proximate individuals. Certain psychological responses of a person undergoing this phase would be: "Why me? It's not fair!" "How can this happen to me?" '"Who is to blame?" "Why would this happen?"*

This anger could be directed inwardly toward the patient himself for not taking better care of his health or toward a situation that may have led to this outcome. More often, the anger is directed at others. Close family and friends can become easy targets. They are often able to provide forgiveness and a safe space for their loved one to vent anger. It's not uncommon for patients to express anger towards us, the medical staff who discover and deliver the diagnosis. I recall one patient who was told his cancer had metastasized. After sitting silently for several minutes, he rigidly got up, ignored our attempts to talk more about it, and walked out of the room. A half hour later, our staff heard that our patient had crashed through the parking lot exit arm without stopping to pay.

3. Bargaining *The third stage involves the hope that the individual can avoid a cause of grief. Usually, the negotiation for an extended life is made in exchange for a reformed lifestyle. People facing less serious trauma can bargain or seek compromise. This is the stage where a negotiation with a patient's higher power commonly takes place. Promises are made to change or to commit to a different life style, if only.*

We have learned to bargain from a young age and often with a payoff. "Please mom, can I just finish watching this movie and I promise I will get my homework done afterwards." When Death's knock is louder than ever, the patient will bargain the extension of life. "Please just let me live long enough to see my daughter get married, and then I will be ready to go."

One of our palliative patients had a goal to attend her daughter's wedding. Her daily visits to our clinic were for radiation treatments to her lower back with the goal of easing her pain. Her cancer had spread to multiple sites and her bone scan showed many "hot spots" where the cancer had spread, and where we had already treated. This lady required weekly blood transfusions to keep her red blood cell count up to a low normal. Every day she arrived for her treatments. No longer having the strength to walk, she required a wheelchair. Her oxygen levels were low and she required the consistency of oxygen support. As she was frail and week, it required two therapists to assist her on the treatment table. She managed to attend the wedding ceremony. Then the following Monday, she asked her oncologist if he could support her attending her grandchild's Junior High School graduation two months away.

4. **Depression** *"I'm so sad, why bother with anything?" "I'm going to die soon, so what's the point?" "I miss my loved one, why go on?" During the fourth stage, the individual despairs at the recognition of mortality. In this state, the individual may become silent, refuse visitors, and spend much of the time mournful and sullen. The patient could withdraw from events and*

participate less and less in life's activities. If this stage is prolonged, without intervention, the person may act on his or her suicidal thoughts.

Our patients experience physical changes due to their disease. Surgery may leave disfigurement with their bodies not even recognizable. A loss of weight or even gaining unwanted pounds adds more misery and sadness. We often see patients after the changes have occurred.

One patient had to be repositioned during her last days of life. It took four nurses and all our strength to do this. I saw a very obese woman whose weight would take a toll on my back as I shifted her from one side to another. When she was settled, her husband, who had been watching us, asked if he could show us something. He reached into his pocket and pulled out his wallet, removing a picture. He paused for a moment and looked lovingly at the photo before he showed us. "This was my wife last year," he tearfully said. I was shocked at the smiling woman, looking back at me. I did not recognize her. A shapely woman in a two-piece swim suit was laughing into the camera. Steroids had bloated her body and removed any evidence of who she once was. It was a powerful lesson to me. This patient had not eaten herself into obesity, nor had she made unhealthy choices. How she now appeared was a product of her treatments. I could not imagine looking into the mirror and not recognizing myself.

5. Acceptance *"It's going to be okay." "I can't fight it, I may as well prepare for it." In this last stage, individuals embrace mortality, or the inevitable future of a loved one or other tragic event. People dying may precede their surviving family members in this state, which typically comes with a calm, retrospective view for the individual and stabilized emotions. When patients arrive at this stage, they can have meaningful conversations with others, as well as assess what's important in their life and what can take place between them and family members, friends, and caregivers.*

During the stage of Acceptance, your patient may appear withdrawn and sleep long hours in the day. This is different from the signs of Depression. In the Acceptance stage, your patient is actually feeling peaceful. He has had the opportunity to look at his life and accept what he has accomplished or what he had not finished. A serenity surrounds him. He may wish to see fewer people, and his interests in the lives of those surrounding him has decreased, along with conversation. His periods of rest are not to escape but to prepare him for the eternal rest that is coming.

Kim in Chapter 11 is my hero for acceptance. A blind teenager, she never questioned what would happen next. She walked every step of her seven-year journey in the moment. I never heard her complain about her situation, or worry about the future. She looked forward to joining her friend and her grandparents. She said they were waiting for her in Heaven. Her laughter never stopped. She trusted the process of life. It was as though she had a secret others were not aware of. I hope I have half her courage when my time comes.

There is no time limit a person spends at a certain stage before moving on to the next. There is also no neat, linear, orderly fashion in which a person moves from denial to acceptance. Patients don't necessarily experience all stages either. Nothing about facing death is predictable. People and their circumstances are never the same. As a nurse, you will want to prepare yourself for a wide range of human responses from your patients and their families who are dealing with dying and death.

As a nurse, my role is not to be my patient's counselor. I know where the line is, and I do not attempt to counsel my patients. Instead, I engage them in a conversation that has them see some possibility of living their lives powerfully while still maintaining some control of themselves. I find supportive counseling invaluable for my patients, and I often suggest this option to them. I want my patients to know they can still be actively living and experiencing peace, even some joy, regardless of their prognosis.

So how do you effectively have a conversation with your patients that leaves them heard, understood, and supported? Every patient is different. Every scenario is different. Your patient is dealing with end of life issues and concerns. He or she is looking to you for support and perhaps some guidance. Trust your intuition. Your instinct will tell you when it is appropriate to move your chair closer to your patient or even hold his or her hand for support. The more experiences you have connecting with your patients, the more confidence you'll have initiating and guiding a conversation that leaves both of you feeling connected and understood. Telling your patients, you don't know how they feel, but that you are sorry for what they are going through, is also more honest than pretending to know how they feel.

In chapter 2, I write about a nurse, Marilyn, that I cared for as she was dying. I could not imagine what she was going through, and I felt helpless not knowing what to say to encourage or support her. It turns out that all she wanted from me was to sit by her bedside and not say anything. Someone just quietly being with her was all she needed. She was simply grateful for my presence. Sometimes saying less is actually saying more.

Patients may also look at you as someone of power or perceived power especially if the patient is vulnerable. There can be negative consequences of crossing boundaries (in terms of professional practice). Physicians may not always be available to relay test results or reorder a prescription to an anxious patient. It may seem like an easy task for you to do and would appear to be supporting your patient's needs. Your regulatory association and your individual institutions may have policies pertaining to boundaries that will ensure you are delivering care and information within your scope of practice. Be familiar with your scope of practice to avoid potential negative consequences.

QUESTIONS TO ASK YOURSELF

1. You are ready to start an infusion of analgesia for your patient and a family member asks if you have the right dose. What is your response?

2. You enter your patient's room, and she is alone, quietly weeping. How would you approach her and what might you say?

3. Your patient has been waiting patiently for their results of the recent MRI they had done. Their appointment with the Physician is a few days away. They ask you for the results. What is in your scope of practice in regards to relaying test results?

CHAPTER 19

SUPPORTING FAMILY MEMBERS OF TERMINALLY ILL PATIENTS

The best support you can give
is not found in a textbook.

AFTER READING THIS CHAPTER

You will recognize opportunities to support families at the bedside.

You will acknowledge and support families who choose to leave the bedside.

GUIDING YOUR PATIENTS AND THEIR LOVED ONES

When patients are nearing the end of their lives, some family members want to stay at their loved one's bedside but find it challenging to do so, for various reasons. Their loved one's loss of consciousness or ability to recognize them may be too distressing. The physical changes that happen during the dying process may also be upsetting. Not everyone has seen someone die before, and being confronted with a sense of duty mixed with fear can bring up many emotions.

As your patient's nurse, you can reassure loved ones that how they are feeling is quite normal. Dying is a process. Not all deaths are peaceful and pain free. Breathing patterns change. The patient's respirations may be shallow or even labored, with periods of no breathing and then, with a gasp, start again. These sounds can be stressful for loved ones to hear. Patients may have lost their ability to control their bowels and bladder, leaving an unpleasant odor in the room. Witnessing a loved one transition from life to death can bring up many emotions. Observing can be stressful on its own, but watching a loved one die and leave this world can add to a family's apprehension. When you share with the family information about the process a person's body goes through as it shuts down various systems, you can address some of their fears and anxieties, reassuring the family that this is a normal process.

One main concern family members often have is why their loved one is not being given any nourishment or water by starting an IV? You can offer them a simple explanation about the dying process, telling them their loved one's body is slowly closing down various organs and that adding fluids now would cause your patient more stress in trying to cope with the extra liquid. Moistening a patient's lips to provide comfort without taxing the body with extra fluids shows families there are other ways to give comfort. As the body is preparing to die, the temperature of the skin gets cooler. Families may express concern about the coolness and mottled appearance of their loved one's arms and legs or hands and feet. Reassuring them that this is a normal progression and providing warm blankets for your patient can comfort the family. Toward the end, stacking rapid inspirations and then a period of silence might occur. The patient may appear to be reaching for air when silently opening and closing his mouth.

Observing these processes occurring can be distressing for families to watch. Ensure your patient is kept comfortable with analgesia. You can also reposition them in the bed and assist loved ones through this difficult time by continuing to explain and reassure family members about the process. Soft lighting and a quiet atmosphere creates a calm, peaceful environment for your patient's transition as well as for their loved ones comfort. You can suggest other ideas to families to contribute to the serenity of the space, such as having their loved one's favorite music softly playing in the room.

For a patient who is no longer able to communicate, encourage family and friends to speak in soothing and comforting ways to their loved one. Sometimes it takes you leading by example to give loved ones permission to communicate in these ways. Before touching your patient, offer a simple explanation about what you are planning to do. Then say something like, "Mrs. Jones, it's Meina, your nurse. I'm going to turn you over on your other side now to make you more comfortable." While gently holding her hand, you can let your patient know that she is not alone and that she is safe. Loved ones are not always aware of what they can do in a situation like this. Your words and actions can demonstrate for the family what they can easily do, but sometimes it takes encouragement and support from you to show them how. Every death is different and every family will have its own level of coping and comfort during this time. Trust your instinct about the best and most appropriate support that they feel comfortable providing.

Even after educating the family about what your patient is experiencing, some may still find it difficult to stay at their loved one's bedside. There may be other circumstances preventing them from staying. Not all employers are sympathetic to their employees' need for time off to be at the bedside of a loved one. Assuring your patient's family member that their loved one will be taken care of in their absence is sometimes the permission they need to leave. Doing so can alleviate the guilt they may feel about leaving, even years afterward. Support their decision to go by providing them with the phone number to the unit. Encourage them to call anytime. It's a difficult choice that families make when leaving their loved one. Guilt may set in after your patient dies. You want to ensure that a family member's decision to leave is supported and free of expectations from anyone.

In Chapter 7, I shared about how my patient's daughter could not stay at her mother's bedside because she had three small children at home. I left a note for the daughter to read in the morning, not only to reassure her about her mother's condition during the night, but also to connect her daughter with the nurse who had been with her mother while she was away resting herself. Months later she expressed her gratitude in knowing that her mother was not alone.

Other family members find it necessary to be present until the very end. They are vigilant, never leaving the bedside. For hours, and sometimes days, they stay waiting for their loved one's last breath. Then they may leave for a quick bathroom break or walk down to the cafeteria to grab a coffee. At that exact moment, their loved one dies. On returning to the patient's room, they are shocked that they missed this last pivotal moment. Guilt, sorrow, or even anger may be their response. They may ask you, "Why? How did this happen when I had been there for so many long hours?" They are asking for answers to unanswerable questions. When this happens, I explain that I have often seen patients pass on when their loved ones have momentarily stepped out of the room. I say, "I believe your loved one has chosen the time to go herself. Perhaps she chose this time to go to spare you from having to watch." Sometimes this gives family members comfort. At the very least, I believe it gives them something to consider. Personally, I think of this type of departure as a gift the patient has given their loved ones, so they don't have to witness that last breath.

One of the most difficult things I find is phoning the family to inform them of their loved one's passing. Giving such intimate news over the telephone is difficult to receive as well as to communicate. Starting the conversation slowly with "I am very sorry to have to tell you this......" can mentally prepare the listener for the news that you are about to tell them. Often the family members are expecting the call, but there are the times when a patient has died sooner than was foreseeable.

Your patient's family will remember the support you've offered them for years to come. I will never forget the kindness of the nurse who took care of my father during his final hours. She would just poke her head around the door of the room and whisper, "Is there anything I can support you with?" We knew we were playing a waiting game, but her willingness to check in regularly and offer help, made me and my family feel we were not waiting alone.

QUESTIONS TO ASK YOURSELF

1. Your patient is dying and family members are exhausted. What support could you offer them?

2. Your patient has died and the family is at home. What could you say on the phone to tell them?

3. Your patient is dying and their breath sounds are rattly and distressing the family. How could you ease the discomfort of the patient's family?

CHAPTER 20

ENHANCING YOUR COMMUNICATION SKILLS

Your competency could be
judged by the words you choose.

AFTER READING THIS CHAPTER

You will enhance your communication
skills during conversations.

You will recognize a patient's ability
to participate in a conversation.

STRENGTHENING COMMUNICATION SKILLS

Often when we are listening to people speak, we are not actually hearing what they are saying. Our attention moves towards silently evaluating and assessing the person or the situation. If the person's words do not coincide with our own beliefs, we may begin to judge rather than listen to what they are communicating. It's not uncommon to formulate our response to what is being said before the other person even finishes. This is how we often communicate and interact with each other. But to actually connect with what another is conveying , we must instead give our full attention to the person's verbal and non-verbal communication.

Fully engaging with your patient will create a more open and trusting relationship. It takes practice to become fully aware of what your patient is saying. Just listen, as much as you possibly can, and only "hear" what the person is expressing, rather than what you think they are voicing. Ask yourself, "What is my patient currently dealing with?" If you are not clear about what your patient or a family member just said, ask them to clarify. You can also repeat back to them in your own words what they said, and ask them if you understood them correctly.

We not only listen with our ears, we also listen with our eyes. Notice the non-verbal cues a patient displays. Mr. V. in Chapter 3 demonstrates a perfect example of a patient's non-verbal communication about his wishes. I did not have to hear any words from him to understand that he did not want to be in that room, nor did he not want to discuss his symptoms of a possible infection. His body language communicated all I needed to see in order to "hear" him.

As health care providers, the nature of our work requires us to become very personal with patients, even when we hardly know them. Moments after meeting a patient, for example, we begin our list of questions that are matter-of-fact to us, but very personal for our patients: "How are your bowels?" "Are you sexually active?" "What medications are you taking?" Our level of questioning becomes quite deep and intimate almost immediately. To get the care they need, patients frequently must have conversations uncomfortable to them. Often they do it grudgingly, realizing this invasion of their privacy is just part of their reluctant journey. Even sitting in the waiting room, they hear their names called loudly. No longer are they just a face in the crowd. Others now know who they are. On nursing and emergency units, their names are displayed boldly with their room numbers. Unless patients are a dignitary or celebrity, there will be no privacy.

In my out-patient unit, there will also be an endless stream of patients waiting to be seen, so I begin by introducing myself, telling them my role and why I am seeing them. I apologize if they have had to wait past their scheduled time because I realize their time is important to them. Frequently they have paid for parking, an added expense. I do not take for granted that they are waiting to see me, and I often tell them this as well. I ensure my patients know that I have time for them if they need it. This lays the foundation of our relationship as patient and nurse.

My goal is to see how my patient is managing right now. I know I cannot have a conversation with someone who is dealing with severe pain. Asking a patient how his bowels are working when the pain he is experiencing is not even allowing him to sit comfortably will not give you access to do a true assessment. His focus will be on his pain and not with general questions.

In addition, I learned long ago not to ask a patient, "How are you feeling, Mr. Jones?"

In response, one man said impatiently to me, "How do you think I am feeling? I'm dying of cancer!"

This man's response taught me that to my patient, the word "feeling" related to his emotional well-being, when in fact, I was wondering how he was feeling physically. He misunderstood my question, but I could understand why.

Now I've learned to ask, "How is your comfort level today, Mr. Jones?"

As caregivers, we assess our patients in many different ways and usually ask them where they get their support. Our best opportunities to make accurate assessments come when we are alone with patients. The answers they give me when their families are present are often different from the responses I get when their loved ones are not in the room. For example, many of my patients will say they get their support from their families when their loved ones are within hearing range. Sometimes I wonder if they are just being polite and trying to reassure their families that what they are doing is enough. It is possible my patients feel they do not want to burden their family by saying how they *really* feel. When I am alone with patients, many of them will respond in a variety of authentic ways: they do not know who to turn to; no one really understands what they are going through; they do not want to burden their families with what they are thinking or what they fear; their religious or spiritual life may be non-existent or it has been a long time since they practiced it; they are feeling alone and emotional on this journey.

Regardless of whether a patient is alone or with his family in the room, I make sure they are aware that there is both psychological and spiritual support available for all of them. I tell them this support team has been trained specifically with techniques and strategies to empower patients and families to move forward. Letting your patients know that other patients have found these support services helpful can have them see that this support is just part of their overall care. They are not being singled out as someone who can not manage. I also emphasize that families and friends, as supportive as they can be, should remain in their role as loved ones and not try to take on the role of counselor.

If my patients or family members are open to receiving counseling or spiritual support, then with the patient's permission, I personally make the call to request this service, because when patients leave the room, they may not make the call themselves. This way, I have helped them make the connection with a vital service, helping to ensure my patient will get a return phone call arranging for an appointment.

Finally, with an influx of immigration from different countries, some of your patients may not speak English. They depend on family members and translators to interpret what they are saying as they describe their condition. Many of these patients are elderly. Not only are they living in a foreign land, they are also being cared for in an unfamiliar health care system. Some family members are reluctant to tell my patient the precise nature of their prognosis or diagnosis. These family translators feel they are protecting their family member because they're concerned that if their loved one finds out about their disease, he or she may give up on life. The best time for a physician to determine a patient's wishes is when an unbiased interpreter is available. The patient may still wish the family to take complete control and report their condition to family members, but at least you and the physician will know for sure that the information has been communicated.

Health care professionals need to understand that various cultures will have differences of opinions about how to care for their family members. By supporting their cultural beliefs, we are supporting the patient. Becoming adversarial about a family's request is not in the best interest of our patients. We need to develop a team approach with the patient, family, and ourselves as medical professionals.

Many of our elderly, non-English-speaking patients are accompanied by their teenage grandchildren to their appointments. If you have questions or concerns that need to be translated and you cannot wait until an interpreter can be found, you may find it necessary to depend on these young family members to assist. Sometimes this can lead to uncomfortable situations. For example, I was not sure who was more embarrassed when I once had to ask a young teenage grandson if his East Indian, non-English-speaking grandmother was having any vaginal discharge. The red-faced grandson and the patient's soft, flustered response had me wish an interpreter could have been readily available, but all three of us did the best we could under the circumstances.

Since that time our institution has implemented an Interpreter Line available for pre-booking or immediate assistance to help in situations like that of the teenager and his grandmother. This has allowed many of our non-English-speaking patients the privacy of a medical consultation.

QUESTIONS TO ASK YOURSELF

1. Your patient does not speak English and is trying to explain something to you. What resources could you access at that moment?

2. Your patient is angry that he has been waiting for his appointment. What can you say to him?

3. Your patient shares his fears of dying and not having enough money for his family. What service can you connect him with that could support him?

CHAPTER 21

DANCING (OR NOT) ON A PATIENT'S DANCE FLOOR

You do not have to dance
to the music you hear.

AFTER READING THIS CHAPTER

You will distinguish boundaries
of professional relationships.

You will realize when your own responses to a
patient's situation require self-care.

LISTENING TO THE MUSIC YOUR PATIENT PLAYS

Sometimes you may meet a certain patient and become connected to him or her at a deeper level than your usual professional nurse-patient relationship. In nursing school our instructor introduced us to the concept of a patient's dance. She told us that all medical staff, as well as all our patients, have a unique dance. My instructor went on to say it was best for the patient, as well as the nurse, to each stay on their own dance floor. In other words, we should keep our relationship with our patient professional at all times and not get personally involved with them. The majority of the time, nurses manage to maintain this relationship.

But you may wonder whether it's always unhealthy for you to shift from a professional to a personal connection with patients for whom you feel a particular kinship. When I did step powerfully on the dance floor of just two patients of mine over the course of my 30-year career, crossing that line gifted me with two amazing relationships that I would otherwise never have had. The loss I felt when these two remarkable young women died was deep and personal. I became a fellow griever alongside their family and friends, rather than a professional supporter.

It would have been very easy for me to step back, remain these two young women's nurse, and not get closely involved with the two families I share about in Chapters 10 and 11. The quality of nursing care I gave would have been the same, regardless of our relationship, but I would probably not have been aware of how or when these two young people's lives ended. By not getting personally involved, I could have saved myself from shedding many tears and feeling many hours of sadness. But I also realized then and now that I became a more caring nurse by getting closer to Taunya and Kim than to all my other patients. I gave them both the support they needed by not only being their nurse, but also by being their friend. In turn, they both gave me the wonderful gift of a deeper awareness and appreciation of my life and those in it. Both girls lived each day to the fullest and showed me, and others, the power of living in the present moment. Through their journeys, they taught me and those around them. Their experiences with terminal illness left a legacy, and I realized I did not have to wait to be dying to leave a legacy myself. I would have missed this valuable lesson, if I had played it safe, followed all the unwritten rules, and stayed off their dance floors.

So how do you decide when to "dance" with your patient or not? The only suggestion I have is to use your best judgement and trust your intuition when considering moving into a more personal relationship with your patients. Remember, when you choose to get personally involved, there's no stepping back into your professional role. You have shared part of yourself and your life with your patient and her family. You are no longer just her nurse, and she is now more than just your patient. You as a nurse have left your role.

In addition, even though you may have chosen not to step on your patient's dance floor, you may still be surprised at the level of sadness you feel for what your patient and the family are experiencing. At times this sadness is actually an accumulation of grief for many patients and many families that you care for, but that you have not had a moment to acknowledge. After all, you will move from one patient's room to another, and you'll carry your work load with you. It's not always easy to separate one experience from another. I remember, one day, thinking, "Is there no one in the world without a cancer diagnosis?"

These feelings of sadness are normal. It's part of being related as a human being to those around us. This is why you went into nursing—to make a difference to those you are caring for. As a nurse, you're not just an instrument of medical delivery. You are entitled to your feelings and emotions. They are an important part of our human experience on earth. I believe it is perfectly fine to show your humanity by sharing with your patients and their loved ones that you are sorry for what they are experiencing. I have often grabbed a box of tissues, not only for my patient, but for myself as well. Revealing your connection, understanding, and compassion shows your patients and their family members that the work you're doing in their behalf is more than just a job for you.

It is equally important for you to be aware that if your own feelings of sadness or grief become overwhelming, it is time to reflect on your own well-being and even seek counseling for yourself. Caring for one patient, and then another, and then another, may not allow you enough time between patients to recover from the most challenging emotions that come with working in the health care field. Keep using your Self-Care Commitment Plan that I discussed in Chapter 15 to help you maintain your physical and emotional well-being. You deserve to be happy and your patients, especially those dealing with difficult diagnoses and depression, will benefit from you remaining strong and steady.

If your grief is prolonged, and you are not releasing the thoughts connected to the difficult experiences you will have as a palliative care nurse, speaking to a professional grief counselor can support you. After all, you are dealing with more grief than the average person does. Your connection with your patient is not at the same level as with your family or friends, but the grief process is certainly the same. Give yourself permission to separate the past from the now, and allow yourself to experience as much joy and satisfaction from your work as possible.

QUESTIONS TO ASK YOURSELF

1. Would it be difficult for you to show your true sadness or grief on a professional level? If so why? If not, can you explain?

2. Have you been in a situation in which you felt called onto the dance floor of one of your patients? How did you respond? If not, how do you think you would react?

3. If you felt you needed additional support for your own sadness or grief, would you seek this? At what point would you seek professional help? If not, why not?

CHAPTER 22

TREAT EVERY PATIENT AS SOMEONE'S LOVED ONE

Everybody deserves to be
treated with respect.

AFTER READING THIS CHAPTER

You will acknowledge patients as individuals with their own life experiences.

You will comprehend that your own responses to your patient's needs can make a profound difference to end-of-life care.

CONNECTING WITH YOUR PATIENTS

The positive impact of the few hours I spent with one patient and her daughter has lasted more than 25 years. I had arrived on duty at 2315 hours and had received a report on the patients who would be in my care during that eight-hour shift. I had my written updates with me as I walked down the hallway assessing those I would be caring for that night. Before I entered the last room, as I stood outside the door, I could hear the sound of quiet, stifled crying. I knew this was the room where an elderly patient was dying. I also knew her daughter was spending the night, so she could be close by her mother's side. Quietly walking into the dimly lit room, I saw a woman in her fifties sitting in a chair by the bed. She was leaning over the bedrails, one arm draped over the rail holding my patient's hand. Her head was resting on her own arm for support as she watched her mother. My patient appeared to be breathing quietly, but not deeply. It was obvious to me that given the sounds of her respirations, she had only a short time to live. I gently touched her daughter's shoulder. She had been so focused on her mother that she had not even heard me enter the room. Quickly, she raised her head, briskly wiping the tears from her eyes and apologized for not hearing me. I reassured her, introduced myself, and asked her if there was anything I could do for her right now?

"You probably think it's silly of me to be crying," she said. "I'm sure you only see an old woman who is ready to die." The next thing she said struck me the most.

"But you know," she cried, "she's still my mom,"

I got the message. No matter what I was seeing between them now, I didn't know the full story of my patient's life or her relationship with her daughter. Nor do I ever know that much about any of my patients' personal journeys through life. I am caring for a person in a hospital bed. I have no connection with their past because I don't know their life history, the loves of their life, their accomplishments, or the sorrows they've endured. All I know is who they are at the moment—a patient with a diagnosis that I am trained to support. This lesson was one of the most powerful lessons I've ever learned as a nurse. I have the privilege of caring for someone's mother, sister, daughter, grandfather, husband, wife, or even best friend. In that room, at that moment, I learned and try never to forget that our patients are much more than just an assignment we get paid to complete. They are unique and precious human beings whom we have the privilege of supporting along one of life's most difficult experiences—their journey toward death.

QUESTIONS TO ASK YOURSELF

1. Take a moment to reflect on your connections with specific patients you are currently caring for.

2. Think about the care you give. Is it the same quality of care you would give to a loved one of your own?

3. What do you say to people when you tell them what you do for a living, and they say, "Oh I could never take care of people who are dying. How do you do it?"

CONCLUSION

The stories I've told in Part I of my book describe key experiences I've had working for 30 years as a palliative care nurse as well as my own life. I hope they have given you an idea about the range of people and situations you may encounter throughout your nursing career supporting terminally ill patients. Each person and each family whose lives I've touched—and who have touched my own—taught me as much about living as they taught me about the process of dying. I'm grateful for their generosity and the lessons I've learned from them.

In Part II, my intention has been to offer enough information and motivation for you to be proactive about optimizing your own self-care as much as you work to optimize the care you give your patients. I trust sharing my experiences will contribute to the success of your career and the privilege of caring for your patients. They will benefit most when you are healthy, strong, and well-prepared to support them and their families, as well as yourself.

This is a poem I wrote to acknowledge all the caregivers who are given the gift of caring for those who are dying.

I AM HERE

I was not there when you became a young adult
Experiencing life that was fun and sometimes difficult.
I was not there when you went on your first date
With that special someone who became your life-mate.
I was not there when your firstborn was placed in your arm
And you promised to protect him from fear and from harm.
I was not there when death knocked and your child died
And no one could relate and alone you grieved and cried.
I was not there as you combed your hair of silver grey
And you reflected how quickly the years slipped away.
I was not there when your life mate took their last breath
And you wondered how you would go on after their death.
Now the knock on the door is for you and you are filled with fear
I want you to know – you are not alone – for I am here.

—*Your Nurse*

Endnotes

1 Thomas Sterling Gordon, PhD and W. Sterling Edwards, MD, *Making the Patient Your Partner – Communication for Doctors and Other Care Givers* (Santa Barbara: Praeger, 1995).

2 "A Quick Biography of Benjamin Franklin," Independence Hall Association, Accessed August 31, 2017, http://www.ushistory.org/Franklin/info/.

3 Susan Kuchinskas, "Meditation Heals Body and Mind," WebMD. 25 Feb 2009.

4 Amy Morin, "Seven Scientifically Proven Benefits of Gratitude that will Motivate You to Give Thanks Year Round," (*Forbes Magazine*, Nov 2014). https://www.forbes.com/sites/amymorin/2014/11/23/7-scientifically-proven-benefits-of-gratitude-that-will-motivate-you-to-give-thanks-year-round/#3043cb3b183c.

5 Deepak Chopra, *The 7 Spiritual Laws of Success*, 9 Nov 1994, http://www.chopra.com/articles/the-7-spiritual-laws-of-success#sm.0000xwfnfp1a7e0mxks1e93jupt5u.

6 Manitoba Nurses Union, "Post-Traumatic Stress in the Nursing Profession: Helping Manitoba's Wounded Healers," February 2016, http://traumadoesntend.ca/#report.

7 Fang Fang, MD, PhD, et al., "Suicide and Cardiovascular Death after a Cancer Diagnosis," (*New England Journal of Medicine*, 4 April 2012).

8 Elisabeth Kübler-Ross, *On Death and Dying* (Macmillan Publishing Co. Inc., New York, 1969).

About the Author

Meina Dubetz was born in the Netherlands and immigrated with her parents to Calgary, Alberta, Canada at age three.

When she was seventeen, Meina began working in a nursing home during the summer where she discovered her passion for caring for patients facing the end of their lives. This experience paved the way for her to become a Licensed Practical Nurse and then later fulfill her dream to become a Registered Nurse. With over thirty years of Oncology Nursing experience in both in-patient and out-patient settings, Meina's connection with her patients, their families, and her peers continue to move and inspire her.

Meina describes her life being balanced by working casual nursing shifts in the summer while spending as much quality time with her three children and four grandchildren as possible. In the winter, Meina and her husband, Art, live in the warmth of the Phoenix area, Arizona where she writes, entertains guests, and makes time for personal growth and professional development opportunities.

Meina earned her Certification in Oncology Nursing in 1996 and her Certification in Gerontology in 2000. She also has a certification as a Death/Life Coach, a certification in hypnotherapy, and is a trained Reiki Master.

When Death Comes Knocking for Your Church Members will be Meina's next book. If you have questions or stories you would like to share about supporting members of your congregation who face end of life circumstances, please email Meina@MeinaDubetz.com

CONTACT

Meina@MeinaDubetz.com

WEBSITE

MeinaDubetz.com

DOWNLOAD THE FOLLOWING FREE RESOURCES FROM MEINA DUBETZ'S WEBSITE:

"Five Leading Causes of Post-Traumatic Stress Disorder in Nurses"
"Five Tips to Calm Yourself at Any Moment: START"
"Template for Self-Care Plan"